A Comparison
OF
Egyptian Symbols
WITH THOSE OF THE HEBREWS

A Comparison

OF

Egyptian Symbols

WITH THOSE OF THE HEBREWS

BY

Frederic Portal

Athens ‡ Manchester

A Comparison of Egyptian Symbols with those of the Hebrews

Published by: Old Book Publishing Ltd

Book Cover Design: Old Book Publishing Ltd

Title of original: A Comparison of Egyptian Symbols with those of the Hebrews

Originally published in 1878

ISBN–10:1-78107-108-X
ISBN–13: 978-1-78107-108-3

EDITOR'S NOTE

A COMPARISON

OF

EGYPTIAN SYMBOLS

WITH THOSE OF THE HEBREWS

By FREDERIC PORTAL.

"The symbols of the Egyptians are like unto those of the Hebrews."
(CLEMENT OF ALEXANDRIA, *Stromates*, V.)

TRANSLATED FROM THE FRENCH,

By JOHN W. SIMONS,

PAST GRAND MASTER OF MASONS, GRAND TREASURER OF THE GRAND LODGE OF NEW YORK,
GRAND TREASURER OF THE GRAND ENCAMPMENT OF THE UNITED STATES, ETC.

NEW YORK:

MASONIC PUBLISHING & FURNISHING CO.,

BARKER, DU LAURANS & DURHAM, 729 BROADWAY.

1878.

EGYPTIAN SYMBOLS

COMPARED TO THOSE OF THE HEBREWS.

CHAPTER I.

PRINCIPLE OF SYMBOLOGY.

THE origin of the science of symbols is lost in the distance of time, and seems to be connected with the cradle of humanity—the oldest religions were governed by it; the arts of design, architecture, statuary, and painting were born under its influence, and primitive writing was one of its applications.

Did symbols exist in spoken, before being translated into written, language? Were primitive words the source of symbols? are the questions on which these researches are based.

The first men, in order to express abstract ideas, borrowed images from surrounding nature; by a surprising intuition, they attached to each race and species of animals, to plants, and the elements, ideas of beauty or ugliness, of good or evil, of affection or hatred, of purity or uncleanness, of truth or error.

Those fathers of the human race did not compare, but they named their ideas from *corresponding objects* in the material world; thus, if they wished to say, the king of an obedient people, they did not compare him to a *bee* governing a submissive hive, but they called him *bee;* if they desired to say filial piety, they did not compare it to the *stork* feeding its family, but they called it *stork;* to express power, they called it *bull;* the power of man, the *arm;* strength of soul, *lion;* the *soul aspiring to heaven,* the *hawk* that sails in the clouds and looks steadfastly at the sun.

Primitive writing, the image of primitive speech, was

entirely composed of symbolic characters, as demonstrated by the examples of China and Mexico, and the symbols we have just cited in Egyptian writing.[1]

If the principle, we have thus assumed, is true, the speech of the first people must have left profound traces of its ambiguities in the most ancient known languages; doubtless, in the lapse of time, figurative expressions passed from tropes to abstractions. The descendants of the patriarchs, in pronouncing the word *bee*, and attaching the idea of a *king* to it, no longer thought of the insect living in a monarchical state, hence arose a change in pronunciation, at first scarcely perceptible, but which, degenerating from tongue to tongue, finally destroyed every trace of symbolism; a dead poetry disinherited the living poetry of preceding ages; comparisons were instituted, and rhetoric took the place of symbols.

This theory results from the following facts: Horapollo teaches the principle of Egyptian symbology when he says that the hawk is the symbol of the soul; for in the Egyptian tongue, the name of the Hawk is Baieth, signifying *soul* and *heart*—Bai, soul, and eth, heart. (Horap. I. 7.)

Thus, in Egypt, symbology rested on the fact that the name of a symbol contained the *idea* or *ideas* symbolized, since the Hawk borrowed its significance from the two roots of its name. To us, the testimony of Horapollo appears positive; is it indisputable?

The knowledge of symbols employed by Champollion, and by the learned of the present day, to decipher Egyptian writings, depends almost entirely on Horapollo; the Rosetta-stone showed the use of those characters mingled with alphabetic writing, by partly confirming the text of the Egyptian *hierogrammat.*

"Hitherto," says Champollion, "I have recognized in the hieroglyphic texts, but thirty of the seventy physical objects indicated by Horapollo in his first book, as symbolic signs of certain ideas; and of these thirty, there

---

[1] According to Champollion, the Egyptians apparently first used figurative and symbolic characters. (*Precis.* 358.) M. Lepsius also thinks that Egyptian writing was, at first, entirely figurative (*Annales de l'Institut de correspondance archeologique,* tom. IX., p. 24 1837.)

are but thirteen—to wit, the *reversed crescent*, the *beetle*, the *vulture*, the *hinder parts of the lion*, the *three vases*, the *hare*, the *Ibis*, the *inkstand*, the *reed*, the *bull*, the *Egyptian goose*, the *head of the Hoopoe*, and the *bee*, which, in reality, appear to have the meaning he attributes to them. But the greater part of the symbolic images, indicated by him throughout his first book, and that part of the second which seems the most authentic, may be found in sculptured or painted pictures, either on the walls of the Temples, Palaces, and tombs, or in manuscripts, on the winding-sheets and coffins of mummies, on amulets, etc." (*Precis*. 348.)

M. Champollion, whether reading manuscripts or in examining other remains, has no hesitation in giving to symbolic forms the signification ascribed to them by Horapollo. The descriptive notice of Egyptian monuments, in the Paris museum, displays the faith of the learned Frenchman in the Egyptian writer. Horapollo could not, then, have been mistaken in announcing as a fact known in his day, that certain signs had certain significations, because the name contained the signification. A meaning may be invented for a symbol, or it may be distorted from that it really possesses; but that an Egyptian writer should suppose so extraordinary a principle as that of homonomy, and that that principle should be false, is ·more than we can admit. This reasoning has appeared conclusive to several learned men who have studied Egyptian writing; among the first of whom, Zoega, author of a celebrated Treatise on Obelisks, recognized it in principle.

" The nomenclature exhibited by Zoega, in his Treatise on Obelisks," says Doctor Dujardin, "admitted a *phonetic* employment of the hieroglyphic signs, in which the characters of the sacred writings performed a part analogous to the figures composing a *rebus*. Horapollo, on whose authority Zoega admitted this fifth mode of expression, gives us only a single example; he shows us the Hawk employed, not *figuratively*, to represent the bird of that name, not as a *trope* to express the idea of elevation, not *enigmatically* to recall the idea of the god Horus, but *phonetically* to designate the Soul. The two names of Hawk and Soul, sounding the same to the ear, these two things, though widely different, being homonyms, as soon as the figure of the hawk was used to designate the name only of that bird, it will be admitted that from that use might result the expression of the idea soul."

"This last mode of expression has been pointed out by Origny, in his Researches on Ancient Egypt, and by Zoega, in his Treatise on Obelisks, as likely to present, if actually made use of, an almost insurmountable obstacle to the interpretation of a great number of hieroglyphic pictures. Every tongue becoming altered by the lapse of ages, it is presumable that the Egyptian could not pass through thousands of years without some changes, without, perhaps, considerable modification; now, in such a labor, the primitive ambiguities are effaced and disappear, while new ones appear in their places. The form and natural qualities of objects do not change; thus modes of expression, founded on that form and those qualities, may be expected to present the same results at different and extremely distant periods of time; but *names* change with time, so that a given figure, which, on account of its name, might symbolize a certain idea at a certain time, might at a future period, by the changes it had undergone, express a very different idea from that intended by the writer."[1]

We admit both the principle and the result deduced from it by Mr. Dujardin, adding, that symbology originated in homonymies, but that the science once established, tongues might alter, without affecting the primitive signification of the symbols. The study of the Coptic proves this fact, since the symbolic ambiguities have, in a great measure, disappeared from the spoken language of Egypt, without affecting the value of the symbols; there have been formed, by chance or otherwise, new homonymies in the Coptic, without giving rise to a new symbology, yet as the principle of the science of symbols was present in the minds of the hierogrammats, it has happened in periods of decay, that the sacred scribes played upon words, with a leaning to riddles or puns; as remarked by Champollion in the inscriptions on the portal of Denderah (Letters from Egypt, page 397); and this appears to confirm our hypothesis.

[1] *Revue des Deux Mondes*, II. part, XXVI., pp. 771, 772.

M. Dujardin concludes that the Coptic, not being the primitive Egyptian, could not reproduce the symbolic homonymies ; to which conclusion we are also led by the logic and study of the facts. Light is here thrown upon the question by the labors of M. Goulianof, whose system, presented in his Essay on the Hieroglyphics of Horapollo, was ardently sustained by the learned orientalist, Klaproth, and attacked by Champollion. This system, partly rests on what the Russian Academician calls *paronomases* or play of words ; he found but eighteen in Horapollo capable of being explained by the Coptic, and several of these were inadmissible.

This labor has been serviceable to science, in proving that Egyptian symbology must have originated in the homonymies, since traces of it are still to be found in the Coptic, and, moreover, that it is useless to seek for a complete explanation of Egyptian symbols in that tongue.

M. Goulianof was himself convinced of this, when he abandoned the *paronomases*, to take up what he called *acrologies*, or explanation of symbols, by the simple use of the identity between the first letter of the name of the symbol and that of the idea symbolized. Finally, no longer finding in the Coptic the explanation of symbols as given by Horapollo, M. Goulianof, in his *Archeologie Egyptienne*, falls into the danger pointed out by Zoega, d'Origny and Dujardin, by undertaking to form, from the Coptic alone, a new symbology in opposition to the testimony of antiquity and the evidence of monuments.

Homonyms exist in all languages, but are they symbols ? *No ;* those of the Coptic tongue are, for the most part, the result of chance, and a few them of, only, manifest the influence of symbology.

M. Goulian of could easily find homonyms in the Coptic, but this fact, reproduced in all tongues, is of no value unless it confirms scientific facts now ; a glance at some of M. Goulianof's explanations will suffice to show that his new system is in manifest opposition to the relations of antiquity and modern discoveries.

Thus, according to Ammianus Marcellinus and Horapollo, the bee, symbol of a king governing an obedient people, would designate impious kings. The white

crown, and the red crown, which, according to the
Rosetta-stone, and all the learned, are the signs of
Upper and Lower Egypt, become the crown of the impious Pharaohs, and the crown spotted with blood.
The beetle would be the apocalyptic symbol of the
grasshoppers coming out of the bottomless pit; finally,
not only would the Pharaohs be impious, but the gods
would transform themselves into devils (Archéologie
Egyptienne, tom. iii.).

We think that the bases of Egyptian science are hence-
forward too solidly established to be destroyed, and that
new discoveries are only to be made, by keeping in the
path already marked out.

Salvolini, in accepting the indisputable facts, and recognizing the principle of Egyptian symbology, gave a
renewed impulse to the science, and, if he did not attain
the end, he, at least, cleared the way; his successive
discoveries bring out the truth of the principle on which
we rest in its full strength. In his work on the "Campagne de Rhamsès," he says : "Here is a fact that has
not yet been established ; we know that a certain like-
ness of an object has been used in the sacred writings,
as the trope of a certain idea ; but I am not aware that
any one has called attention to the phonetic expression
of the *proper name* of that object, as it is used in spoken
language, representing sometimes in written language
the trope of the same idea, of which the isolated image
of the object was once the symbol. Such is the origin,
in my mind, of the signification of *strength*, often given
in the texts to the word ⲩⲉⲩⲛⲉⲩ *thigh of an ox ;* though
led to this conclusion by a multitude of examples, I
will only cite one. It is known by Horapollo's text,
that, in Egypt, the vulture was the emblem of victory
(I. ii), the name of that bird, as found in inscriptions, is
always written ⲛⲡⲉⲟⲩ ; the Coptic ⲛⲟⲩⲣⲉ. Now, this
same name has frequently been employed, either in the
funeral Ritual, or other writings, to express the idea, *to
conquer* or *victory*, only in the latter case it has a second
determinative, the *arm holding a tomahawk* . . . . .

"Such a fact has nothing extraordinary in its nature ;
but we should certainly be surprised upon discovering
that, though in the ancient Egyptian texts there exists
a certain number of *symbolic words*, such as I have just

designated, the Coptic tongue has scarcely a trace of them." (Salvolini, *Campagne de Rhamsès*, p. 89.)

Salvolini, in the *Analysis of Egyptian Texts*, expresses his ideas in a more complete manner, and acknowldeges for the Coptic tongue a more symbolic character than he at first supposed. He admits in principle, that a word may have for a determinative, a sign, the name of which is the same as the word accompanying it, though it ir no wise represents the same idea; in translating his thoughts, we add, that symbolic determinatives obtain their value from homonymies. The following passage is too important to be passed in silence : " The admission, on my part, of an opinion, such as that I have just announced relative to the origin of the use of two different characters as tropes of the idea *race* or *germ*, will not fail to surprise those who know how constantly it has been disavowed by my illustrious master.[1] If we may believe the dogmas sought to be established by him in his last work, the signs employed by the Egyptians as tropes, are reduced, as to their origin, to the four following processes, pointed out by Clement Alexandrinus : first, by *synecdoche ;* second, by *metonymy ;* third, by *metaphor ;* fourth, by *enigmas ;*[2] but I must acknowledge, according to my own experience, that a brief progress in the study of hieroglyphic writing will demonstrate the insufficiency of the four methods above cited for explaining the multitude of symbolic characters unceasingly employed by the Egyptians. The learned philologist himself, who, at the time of publishing his *Précis*, had already acknowledged the four processes announced in his hieroglyphic grammar for the formation of symbolic signs, admits in the latter part of his work,[3] *that there only remained to be found a method for knowing the value of symbolic characters ; and that,* he adds, *is the obstacle which seems destined to retard a full and entire knowledge of hieroglyphic texts.* I am persuaded that the method, which the late Champollion desired to have discovered, of finding the origin of the great number of

[1] This passage seems to allude to Goulianof's system, attacked by Champollion.

[2] Vide *Egyptian Grammar*, p. 23.

[3] *Précis du Système Hiéroglyphique*, p. 338, and 462-3. 2d edition.

1*

Egyptian characters employed as tropes, which could not be explained by Clement of Alexandria's process—that this method, I say, is found in the new principle I have just applied to explain the determinative characters of the word ROT *germ.* I here give my formula of the principle :

"*As every hieroglyphic image has a corresponding term in spoken language, a certain number of them have been taken as signs of the sounds to which they answer, an abstraction from their primitive signification. The hieroglyphic characters belonging to this singular method of expression, as all other signs employed in Egyptian writing as tropes, have been employed either* by themselves, or following *words.*" Analysis, p. 225.

As an application of this system, Salvolini shows that the Egyptian word IRI, *to do,* is usually represented in the text by the isolated image of an *eye,* because, according to Plutarch and the monuments, the name of the eye is also IRI. In like manner, the *calf's snout* signifies *he who is at* or *in,* because the name of snout or *nose,* FNT or FENT, alludes to the word PENTE, *he who is at* or *in.* The character *hatchet* signifies *God,* because the word TER designates a *hatchet* and a *God.*

The idea of a statue was represented by the god Toth, because the name of *Toth* formed the word *statue.* (Rosetta-stone.)

The god Toth, protector of *Hermopolis magna,* had for a title in the inscriptions the sign *lord,* and the sign of the number *eight,* because, in Egyptian, the name *Hermopolis* signifies *eight.*

The goddess Neith had for a symbolic name a kind of weaver's loom, because the same resemblance existed between the name *Neith* and the loom *nat.*

A species of aquatic bird was the sign for the idea of doctor, because on the monuments the name of the bird is SINI, and in Coptic the word SEINI signifies doctor.

The *finger* represents the number ten thousand, and TEB signifies *finger,* and TBA ten thousand.

"I do not know," adds Salvolini, "whether the few examples I have submitted to the reader in proof of the new facts, the existence of which, I believe, I have discovered in the system of Egyptian writing, will be sufficient to convince him. As to myself, thoroughly cou-

vinced of the reality of the principle I seek to establish—
a conviction founded on results obtained from the application of this principle to the interpretation of a large
number of texts—·I frankly avow that, from the moment
I first suspected its existence, the symbolic portion of
Egyptian writings—a portion which, it may be said,
Champollion left untouched, and which it is, nevertheless, necessary to know—appeared to me in its true
meaning." (Analysis, p. 233.)

Following this decisive testimony, we present that of
a man whom the learned of Europe justly consider as
one of the actual representatives of Egyptian science.

Mr. Lepsius, in his letter to Rosellini, endeavors to
find the means of recognizing the signification of figurative signs, and he assigns ten leading principles for
attaining that end. The first eight, which we reproduce
here as having adopted them in our researches, are :

1. The actual representation of the object, taken with
its proper meaning ;

2. The images or pictures that the character accompanies ;

3. Explanations of Greek or Latin authors ;

4. Ancient translations ;

5. The context itself ;

6. The phonetic group accompanying the sign ;

7. The *variants* in different texts ;

8. The figurative signs employed as initials to certain
groups, of which the balance is phonetic.

In developing this last principle, that of initial signs,
Mr. Lepsius says :

" These are signs which were also frequently employed alone, and with a figurative meaning, but which, at
the same time, served to represent all words or parts of
words containing the same letters, though they often
had a very different meaning. We have several times
met with the same use of purely figurative characters.
The basket is pronounced ᚾᚼ, and designates as well
Lord ᚾᛖᚼ, as *all* ᚾᛁᚼᛁ."[1]

From these last passages of Salvolini and Lepsius, it
is easy to perceive that the labors of these learned men

---

[1] *Annales de l'Institut de correspondance Archéologique;* Rome, 1837,
p. 26 and 51, tome ix.

depend, in part, at least, on homonymies, and are, consequently, in accordance with the theory of the Russian
academician; only M. Goulianof wants to find the
explanation of the symbols in the Coptic alone, while
Salvolini and Lepsius look for it also in the hieroglyphic
texts.   The natural consequence of this last principle
was, the division of the Egyptian tongue into two dialects, the *Egyptian of the monuments* and the *Coptic*, answering to the *sacred tongue* and the *vulgar tongue* of
Manetho.

Listen again to Mr. Lepsius: "The Egyptians, he
says, had two distinct dialects, to wit: the ancient clas-
sic and sacred dialect [ἱερὰ γλῶσσα,[1] ἱερὰ διάλεκτος[2]], and the
popular dialect [κοινὴ διάλεκτος[3]] ; the *sacred* writing as
well as the *popular hieratic* writing always present the
sacred dialect; and the *popular epistolographic* writing as
well as Coptic literature present the popular dialect.[4]

The facts and reasonings, on which Mr. Lepsius founds
his opinion, appear to be firmly established; this division
of the two tongues explains why the Coptic cannot be
used to interpret the symbols, while it is partly found in
the sacred tongue;[5] yet there is but little difference
between these two sacred and profane dialects, and if
the first presents a large number of words not found in
the second, still the language of the monuments is far
from affording a complete explanation of the symbols.

We have no doubt, however, that new labors, undertaken with a view of discovering symbolic words in hieroglyphic texts, will lead to important results; but to
accomplish this it will, doubtless, be necessary to consult
the origin of Egyptian symbols.

It is now generally acknowledged that the Egyptian
religion and system of writing were borrowed from
Ethiopia.[6]

The necessary consequence of this fact, and what pre-

[1] Maneth. ap. Jos. C. Ap. p. 445.
[2] Maneth. ap. Syncell. Chron. p. 40.
[3] Maneth. ap. Jos. lib. i.
[4] *Annales de l'Institut de corres. Archéol.*, ix., 18 ; and appendix, p. 67
Salvolini, Camp. de Rham., p. 91, and Traduc. de l'Obelisque, p. 10.
[5] Of the eight examples of symbolic homonymies cited from Salvolini,
four are found in the Coptic ; they are the *status*, *eight*, the *loom* and the
finger.
[6] Champollion-Figeac, *Egypte ancienne*, p. 28, 34, 417.

cedes it, is, that the language of Ethiopia contained an explanation of the symbols; could it, in fact, be admitted that the inventors of a system of writing, based on language, should have made use of a strange tongue to express their ideas? The Egyptians accepted the Ethiopian symbols with the signification that had been given them when writing originated. We have already said that symbols depended on language at the period of their formation; and that the system of symbology having been established, language might vary or completely change without making the least alteration in the primitive meaning of the image. Thus the Egyptians might have adopted the Ethiopian symbology entire, without their language having the least relation to the significance of the symbols; still, it is more than probable that Egypt received a part of the Ethiopian words on which the symbols were founded, or at least that the written language of the Egyptians acquired a symbolic character foreign to the common tongue.

No people ever exercised a commanding influence on the civilization of another people without imposing on them a portion of their language; the Ethiopians must have left profound traces of their religious influence in the sacred tongue of Egypt, while this influence on the vulgar dialect must have been much more circumscribed.

An apparent confirmation of this opinion is, that the wordso f the sacred tongue, not found in the Coptic, exist in part in the languages coming from the same stock as the Ethiopian, and that the explanation of Egyptian symbols is also found in these tongues.

Let us here listen to the Egyptian priest, Manetho, explaining the names of pastors or *hykschos :* he says that the word *ϒΚ, King,* belongs to the *sacred tongue, ἱερὰν γλῶσσαν;* while *ΣΩΣ,* pastor, belongs to the *vulgar tongue, κοινὴν διάλεκτον.*

The word *ΣΩΣ* is found in the Coptic with the signification given it by the priest Sebennyt, ϣⲱⲥ *pastor;* the word *ϒΚ, king,* exists on the monuments of the Pharaohs, and is missing from the Coptic; with Mr. Lepsius, we here find a proof that the Coptic was the common, and the hieroglyphic inscriptions the expression of the sacred, language.

The word רK does not exist in the Ethiopian, but is found again in the *Hebrew*, a language having the same origin; the word רK, recognized on the obelisk of the Luxor [1] by Salvolini, is described by the *pedum* and *angle*, which group, transcribed in Hebrew characters according to Champollion's alphabet, gives the word חק a *law*, a *decree*, חקק a *legislator*, a *sovereign*, or king moderator, as translated by Salvolini.[2]

This word is at the same time symbolic, that is, founded on homonymy, since it signifies in Hebrew a *sceptre* and a *sovereign*, and that the sceptre is the sign of the idea *king moderator*. The intimate relations existing between the Ethiopian and Hebrew languages cannot be denied. Wansleben has brought together five hundred roots that are the same in Ethiopian and Hebrew, independent of other analogous languages; this work is printed in Ludlolf's Ethiopian dictionary (p. 475 et seq.); the traveler Bruce, also, noticed this resemblance, (tome ii, p. 267), and the learned Gesenius consecrated it in his lexicon.

An historical reason may here be found for the facts sought to be established in these researches: The Hebrew and the Ethiopian sprung from a common source, as philology proves; one of these dialects we find preserved in its purity in the Pentateuch, while the Ethiopian language has undergone many changes, either by the different migrations of people in Ethiopia, or the lapse of time; we need not, therefore, be astonished to find explanations in Hebrew not in the Ethiopian.

A fact already noticed, but not explained, is, that Egyptian words exist, are reproduced in Hebrew, but are not found in Coptic; Mr. Lepsius uses this observation to explain one of the Egyptian names of the horse, סוס *sus* (Lepsius, *Annales*, ix, 56). I find in the same work the word *scher*, which does not exist in the Coptic, and which Lepsius translates by *reign* (Annales, pl. A, col. c); the Hebrew explains it, for שר *scher* signifies a *prince*, a *king*, a *governor*.

Laying aside here all relation between the Egyptian

---

[1] Façade, Champs-Elysées, first inscription under the banner on the left; Salvolini, Explanation of the obelisk.

[2] *Campagne de Rhamses*, p. 16.

and Hebrew languages, we desire to establish that even if it were demonstrated that the complete signification of the symbols could be found in the Egyptian, and that there was a single word the same in the languages of Moses and the Pharaohs, these two languages, strangers to each other, but animated by the same symbolic genius, would each give to the same physical objects the same moral signification.

The different authorities cited have sufficiently enlightened us, I think, as to the principle of Egyptian symbology; it now becomes necessary to inquire whether this symbolic character belongs to the Hebrew.

Not only all the names of men in Hebrew, but those of quadrupeds, birds, fishes, insects, trees, flowers, and stones are significant. Hebrew scholars require no proof of this; for they are not unacquainted with the learned and voluminous treatise of Bochart on the animals mentioned in the Bible.

This principle of significant names, recognized and adopted as true by the celebrated Gesenius, and by all lexicographers before him, is not to be denied, but its application being purely arbitrary, and having been undertaken without any definite purpose, has furnished science with no useful result.

Bochart, ignoring the principle of symbology, only sought and found purely arbitrary significations in the names of animals; distorting the Hebrew roots according to his fancy, he repels the moral significance they naturally present, because he does not understand the relation that may exist between an animal and a philosophical idea; when this relation is too evident, he gives it, as it were, in spite of himself; thus he cannot deny that the *vulture* signifies *mercy*, and the *mole* the *world*.

The Hebrew, then, has an evident imprint of symbology, since it gives moral significance to material objects. Before drawing a conclusion from this remarkable fact, let us resume the foregoing deductions. Egyptian symbols, founded on homonymies, together with their religion and system of writing, were borrowed from Ethiopia. We have just said that the Hebrew and Ethiopian were derived from a common source, and we are led, in conclusion, to seek whether the Hebrew will afford an explanation of Egyptian symbols.

The question thus presented, can be resolved but in two ways: by the testimony of the writers of antiquity, and by the application of Hebrew to hieroglyphic symbols.

Clement of Alexandria, the father of modern Egyptian science, says, in express terms, that, *touching mysterious things, the symbols of the Egyptians are like unto those of the Hebrews.* Ὅμοια γοῦν τοῖς Ἑβραϊκοῖς, κατά γε τὴν ἐπίκρυψιν, καὶ τῶν Αἰγυπτίων αἰνίγματα.[1]

The authority of Clemens Alexandrinus cannot be doubted; for his testimony is the foundation on which Champollion and the Egyptologists erect their systems of interpreting Egyptian writings. Clemens Alexandrinus, fortified with Bible reading, could not have produced so extraordinary an assimilation for a Christian and Egyptian, without being in possession of proofs of the truth of his assertion; in the Bible and the Hebrew only may we seek for an explanation of Egyptian symbols.

Whether this interpretation appear true or false, it cannot be affirmed nor denied without proofs; in questions of this nature, the argument is subordinate to the facts, and to facts alone we appeal.

The first result of this system would be, to give the explanatory method of Egyptian symbols that Champollion asked for in his *Précis;*[2] Salvolini, in his Analysis of Egyptian texts (p. 225); and that Lepsius endeavored to find in ten different principles. The second would be to consider the Hebrew, if not entirely, at least in a great measure, the expression of primitive symbology. We shall apply this principle to the symbolic colors in the third chapter of this essay. Finally, the third and most important result would be, the application of the principle of symbology to the most symbolic of all books, *the Bible.*

It appears evident to us, that if the Hebrew explains the symbols of Egypt, and explains those emblems that

---

[1] Stromat. lib. V. p. 566, ed. Sylburg.—In this passage, Clement of Alexandria seems to allude to the double meaning of words, since the dictionaries translate ἐπίκρυψις by *ænigmaticus sermo*, and αἴνιγμα by *ambages verborum.*

[2] *Précis,* p. 338 and 462-3, 2d edition.

were the same among all the nations of antiquity, it should also contain the explanation of those biblical images that the learned Lowth and all other Hebrew grammarians have failed to interpret.

In the fourth chapter, we shall give direct proof that the sacred writers used homonymies, and confirm our deductions by the testimony of Hebraists.

It is necessary to add, in this place, a few remarks on the manner in which we shall proceed in these researches.

Egyptian writing neglects the vowels, and is completely identified by this fact with Hebrew writing without vowel-points. Such is the first and greatest discovery of Champollion—a discovery on which all others are based.[1] In these researches, the points in Hebrew writing can, therefore, be of no use, and are consequently omitted. But it is not alone on account of the identity between Hebrew and Egyptian writing that we recognize the necessity of neglecting the vowel-points in homonymies. Hebraists teach us the same method in seeking for roots, since they derive one word from another, presenting the same letters, without regard to differences of pronunciation, marked by vowel-points, which method we shall employ as it is employed on each page of Gesenius' dictionary.

Thus, the homonymy is to be established on the written, and not on the pronounced word; for this I shall further appeal to the testimony of the celebrated Heinsius, who, in interpreting a passage of the Gospel of St. John, says that the sacred writer alludes to the double meaning of the Syriac word בכל *cabbel* and כבל *cebal*, pronounced differently, but of which the letters are the same. We shall recur to this passage in the applications to the Bible (chap. iv).

As this method of neglecting the points may appear arbitrary to some readers, it is necessary to explain it.

At the time when writing was invented, all words written alike had probably the same pronunciation; at a later period, revolutions occurred in languages, the different significations of a word were distinguished by

---

[1] Champollion, *Précis du Système Hiéroglyphique*, second edition, p. 111.

different pronunciation on the vowels, and finally, when these changes extended to a majority of words in the Hebrew, there was felt a necessity of recurring to the vowel-points—an invention going back, at the furthest, to Esdras. Traces of this revolution in the Hebrew are equally evident in the *quiescents*, that is, the old vowels, which, though in pronunciation in Moses' day, have finally been left out of it; as is the result of the concordance of several words and proper names to be found in the Bible, on the monuments of Egypt, and in Greek authors.

In the succeeding chapter we shall give an explanation of fifty symbolic signs, as they result from the testimony of the *Hebrew, Horapollo,* and the *monuments;* we might easily have multiplied the number of these examples, but it has seemed to us that for the reader the best demonstration of the truth of this method was to make new discoveries. Thus we have neglected those signs that may be considered figurative; *smoke* signifying *fire*, the *arm* designating *strength*, the *ladder*, the *assault*, etc. (Horapollo). These significations, which may also be found in the Hebrew,[1] are, nevertheless, not a proof of the symbolic character of that language, since these images are the rhetorical tropes of all people.

There is a large number of Egyptian symbols, the Hebrew name of which I have not been able to find; thus, among animals, the *Ibis*, the *Oryx*, the *Swan*, the *Elephant*, the *Pelican*, etc., named by Horapollo, cannot be explained.

In Horapollo, as in the anaglyphs or symbolic pictures, there exist sacred myths that language fails to give a direct explanation to, as the fable of the ape and its two little ones—one, carried in front, it loves and kills, the other, carried behind, it hates and nourishes. (Horapollo II., 66.)

The cynocephalus ape was in Egypt, as in India, the symbol of regeneration,[2] of the passage from the state of an animal to that of man, and from death to eternal

---

[1] זדוע *arm, strength;* and סלם *a ladder*, and סללה, *ramparts thrown up by the besiegers*, from the root סלה, *to elevate, to set up*, as in French *echelle* and *escalader* are formed from the Latin root *scala*.

[2] *Symbolic Colors,* p. 199.

life ; it is on this account that, when in a sitting posture, it represents the two equinoxes (Horap. I., 16), that is, the state of equilibrium between light and darkness, between good and evil, truth and error, or between brute and man : the funeral ritual represents the ape *seated* on the scale for judging souls.

The ape represented souls traversing the circle of purification before entering the field of truth ; which we also learn from its Hebrew name קוף, an *Ape*, and *to form a circle, achieve a revolution.*

The explanation of this myth becomes easy ; the little one that the ape carries on its breast, that it loves and kills, represents those good sentiments, those virtuous actions that we love, that conscience ever presents to our sight, and yet which we kill in our hearts ; the young one that the ape carries on its back, which it hates and nourishes, symbolizes those evil sentiments, those perverse actions, which we should ever repel, which in our consciences we hate, and yet which we cherish, as it were, in spite of ourselves.[1] These explanations, though more or less probable, I shall neglect, as not necessarily connected with these researches.

In concluding these preliminary observations, I must add, that several attempts to interpret the Egyptian monuments by the Hebrew, have led to no scientific result, because they were, doubtless, founded on two capital errors : first, that the language of Moses was that of the Pharaohs ; and, secondly, that the hieroglyphics formed a series of symbols.

The principle of Egyptian symbology, laid down by Horapollo and taught by Zoega, is recognized even by those authors who depend on the Hebrew, as Lacour of Bordeaux and Janelli of Naples ; it was desired to make a triple application of it, to the Hebrew, to Horapollo and the monuments, but I believe it has never been accomplished.

Symbology, being the most mysterious, must have been the last part of the Egyptian writings discovered ; it being necessary to understand the Egyptian language and system of writing before being able to penetrate

[1] St. Paul says : " For the good that I would do, I do not ; but the evil which I would not, that I do." (Epistle to the Romans, vii. 19.)

the sanctuary. Science had to follow the route taken by the Egyptian initiates. Clemens Alexandrinus says they first learned epistolographic writing, then hierarchical, and, finally, the hieroglyphic, containing symbology. It was in this manner that the labors of Sylvester de Sacy and Akerblad were first directed to epistolographic writing ; that, at a latter period, Champollion deciphered the hierarchical and hieroglyphic writings : and that, in our day, we have to find again the elements of Egyptian symbology. The principle being already known and acknowledged by science, the enlightened critic will not, of course, refuse to apply it to hieroglyphic language, as Salvolini has done, and to the Hebrew, as I propose to do in this essay.

CHAPTER II.

BEE.

THE bee was the symbol of an *obedient people*, because, says Horapollo, it alone, of all animals, had a king (Horap. I. 62).

Champollion gives to the bee the signification, *king of an obedient people* (Amm. Marcell. XVII. 4).

---

[1] To facilitate research, the symbols are arranged in alphabetical order. The dictionaries cited are, for the Hebrew, those of *Gesenius,* 1833; Rosenmüller, Vocab. appended to Simon's Bible, *Hale,* 1822; *Moser, Guarin,* and the Thesaurus of *Robertson ;* for the Coptic, *Peyron's* Lexicon.

Note.—The alphabetical order, it will be understood, applies to the French.

The Abydos tablet shows numerous examples of the use of this sign, and confirms the meaning attributed to it.

The Hebrew name of the bee is דבורה DBURE (Gesenius), or דברה DBRE (Guarin).

דבר DBR signifies *to administer*, *to govern*, *to put in order*, to act like a swarm of bees.[1]

The same root דבר DBR has the further meaning of *discourse, word, λόγος, sentence, precept of wisdom;* it is also the verb *to speak*. Finally the name of the bee in the plural feminine דברות DBRUTH, signifies *words, precepts* (Gesenius).

The bee was the symbol of *royalty* and of *sacred inspiration*, honey represented *initiation* and *wise discourses*, (*Symbolic Colors*, p. 83).

The bee was consecrated to the kings of Egypt, and they were designated by it on the monuments, not only on account of the relation that might exist between the government of that people and bees, but, also, because their kings were *initiates*, and governed by *sacred inspiration*, for they were priests.

ASS.

The Egyptians represented *the man who had never been out of his country by the onacephalus* (head of an ass), (Horapollo I. 23).

The Hebrew language furnishes the explanation of this symbol, since עיר OIR, the *young ass*, signifies a *city*, a *place* (Gesenius).

The other name of the ass, חמור HEMUR, or HEMR חמר, is formed of the word חמה HEME, *to surround with a wall* and חומה HEUME, the *wall surrounding a city*. These Hebrew synonyms, reproducing the same homonyms, demonstrate the truth of our theory.

The ass was consecrated to Typhon, the genius of

---

[1] This insect, says Moser, was called דבור on account of its admirable government; we are rather of the opinion that the art of governing borrowed its name from the bee. (Bochart, Hieroz. II., 502.)

evil, represented by russet color (Symbolic Colors, p. 257), and the name of the *ass* חמר HEMR signifies to *blush, to be inflamed ;*[1] the root of this word is חם *hem* (Ham,) an Egyptian proper name according to the Hebrew and the monuments (See article *crocodile*). According to Plutarch, this name also signified *blackness* and *heat*, חום HEUM signifies *black* (Plutarch *De Isid.* Gesenius;) it forms the word חמס HEMS, *violence, injury, rapine.*

The ass was the symbol of ignorance united to wickedness or goodness : חמר HEMR, the brown ass, represented vicious ignorance; the *white female ass* (Jud. v. 10), was the emblem of ignorance united to goodness and candor, צחרה.

This good or bad ignorance was that of the profane. The ass represented the stupid people of Egypt, חם *Ham,* who, materially, never left the limits of their hordes, and, morally imprisoned in the bonds of error and prejudice, never acquired a knowledge of the mysteries revealed in the initiation.

The white she-ass represented man, not yet possessed of spiritual knowledge, but capable of acquiring it; the story of Alpulée develops this myth in a most ingenious manner; man, whose affections and ideas are strongly bound up in material life, is metamorphosed under the figure of an ass; he travels for a considerable period, arrives in Egypt, where he recovers the human form by initiation. The ass of Silenus, that carried the beverage of eternal youth, changed it for a few mouthfuls of water, (Noël, Dict. de la Fable), emblematical of the profane, preferring the knowledge of the world to those springs of living water that never dry up.

M. Lenormant, in his researches on Horapollo, says the book of that *hierogrammat* has evident marks of interpolation, and that the onacephalus is an invention of the Greek translator Philippe : *As far as I know,* says he, *the ass's head has not been found among the hieroglyphics ; but Egyptian travelers! men ridiculed in that country for never having quitted it ! evidently such ideas are as contrary as possible to the spirit of Ancient Egypt.* (Lenormant, Recherches sur Horapollo.)

---

[1] In like manner עיר, the *ass* and *city*, signifies, also, *to be inflamed,* the *heat of anger,* and an *enemy* (Gesenius).

In fact, the Egyptians had the greatest horror of strangers, as the hieroglyphics incontestably prove (*Vide* Salvolini, Camp. de Rhamsès, p. 15 ; and Champollion, Egypt. Grammar, p. 138). But Horapollo does not say that the onacephalus was the symbol of a man who had never been out of Egypt, but of one who had never quitted his *native country*, his city, or his residence : Ἰνθρωπον τῆς πατρίδος μὴ ἀποδημήσαντα.

If the ass's head had not yet been recognized among the hieroglyphics, that animal would be found in the Hebrew with the signification assigned to it by Horapollo, and in our system this proof would be a convincing one ; but the figure of the ass was stamped on the cakes offered to Typhon, the genius of evil and darkness : finally, this animal in the hieroglyphics is one of the forms of Seth or Typhon, of which Champollion gives us a drawing at p. 120 of his Grammar.

Typhon was sometimes represented with an ass's head, as the following vignette, engraved after the manuscript

of Leyde, published by Leemans, proves.[1] This personage, bearing on his breast the name of *Seth*, and on the legend that of the *ass* ΙϹΩ, appears to us to·be related to the *onacephalus* of Horapollo.

MOUTH.

In the hieroglyphic texts, the mouth is the determin-

---

[1] *Leemans*, Leyde's Egyptian Monuments, p. 15 and 16 ; and Letter to Salvolini, p. 5.

ative and symbol of *door* (Egyptian Grammar, p. 80 and 205); it also designates the idea of *part, portion, fraction* and that of *chapter* (Idem, p. 243).

The Hebrew word פה PE signifies *mouth, door,* a *part,* a *portion.*

And we find in Coptic, ⲢⲞ *mouth, door, chapter, portion,* ⲗⲁ *mouth, door.*

BUNCH OF REEDS.

Champollion says, in his Grammar (p. 128), that the *names of women, except those of Egyptian queens, are terminated or accompanied by a bunch of flowers.*

The bouquet is formed of the flowers of the papyrus; אבה ABE, the *papyrus,* the *reed,* forms the word אהבה AEBE: the *woman loved,* אהב AEB, *love.*

The bunch of papyrus is also the generic determinative of all the names of *plants; herbs,* and *flowers* (Egyptian Grammar, p. 88).

אב AB, *green things, grass,* is the root of אבה ABE, the *papyrus.*

GOAT.

The goat was the symbol of sharp hearing (Horapol., II. 68).

עז oz, a *goat,* and אזן AZN, an *ear:* according to Gesenius, the letters ע o, and א A, are often confounded in Hebrew; that celebrated Hebraist particularly points out the root עזן OZN, as necessarily the same as אזן AZN (Lex. p. 752). Consult the article *Ear.*

STORK.

The Egyptians represented filial piety by a stork; because, says Horapollo, after having been fed by its

2

parents, it does not leave them, but cares for them to
extreme old age (Horap., II. 58).

הסירה HESIDE, the *stork*, the *pious*, the *grateful* (Gesenius).

BRAIDED BASKET.

According to the Rosetta inscription, the basket expressed symbolically the idea of *master* or *lord.*   On
the painted monuments this basket appears to be woven
from various colored reeds (Champ. Gram., p. 26–27).
Champollion also gives to this sign the signification of
the idea *all* (Gram., p. 279, *et passim*).

כלוב KLUB, a *basket woven from reeds* (Gesenius), is from
the root כל KL, *all*, and כלל KLL, *to crown.*

This basket is the *sacred fan,* which was also woven
from willow (Rolle, Culte de Bacchus, I. 29).

כברה KBRE, a *fan*, forms כביר KBIR, *powerful, great ;* נפה
NPE, a *fan*, forms נפילים NPILIM, *powerful men, heroes, lords,
Titans.*

Thus, all the synonyms of the word fan or basket
produce the same homonymies.   The word נפה NPE,
basket and *sieve,* is likewise found in the Egyptian ϣⲃ
basket, which forms ϣⲉⲃ *lord* and ⲛⲓⲃⲥ *all.*

The *fan* became the symbol of the idea *master* or *lord,*
because it was that of the purification of souls.

" The initiations called *Teletes,*" says Mr. Rolle (Ibid,
p. 30), " being the commencement of a better life, and to
become the perfection of it, could not take place till the
soul was purified ; the fan had been accepted as the
symbol of that purification, because the mysteries purged
the soul of sin, as the fan cleanses the grain."

Thus John the Baptist said of the Messiah that he has
the fan in his hand and will purge his floor. (Luke,
iii. 17.)

ROOK.

According to Horapollo, *conjugal union* was repre-
sented by two rooks (Horap., II. 40), and the word ערב
ORB, signifies a *crow*, a *rook*, and to be *conjugally united*
(Gesenius).

ערב ORB, is also the name of the setting sun and the shadow of darkness ; in Egyptian cosmogony, night was the mother of the world, on which account marriage was celebrated among the Athenians during the night (Symbolic Colors, p. 172).

A man who had lived to a sufficient age, was repre sented by a dead rook ; this bird, adds Horapollo, lives a hundred years (II. 89). The name of the rook, ערב ORB, designates sunset, symbol of the natural end of every period. The dead rook was the sun having set.

HORNS.

On the monuments, the horns are the sign of the idea, *to be radiant, refulgent, to shine,* because, says Champollion, the Eastern people found a marked analogy between the horns and the rays of the sun (Egypt. Gram., p. 359 and 360). In writing those lines he had, doubtless, in mind the significations of the Hebrew word קרן QRN, which signifies a *horn, to be radiant, resplendent, to shine ;* for the Coptic word ⲧⲁⲡ , a *horn,* does not signify to shine, and the word ϩⲱⲡ signifies to *hide,* to *cover,* and a *horn.*

MANGER.

" The hieroglyphic name of the city of Thebes, has a quarter circle for a determinative symbol, of which the curved part is presented in a contrary direction to the writing. The explanation of this symbol had long been sought, when at last the flotilla, on board of which was Champollion's scientific expedition, sailing toward Nubia, perceived on shore a row of high mangers, formed of twisted straw and river-mud, a side view of which presented the half circle of the Theban symbol. These mangers were intended for large herds of cattle. It was then recollected, that in fully developed texts, there was often seen a bull placed before the symbol of the city of Thebes. A manger was henceforth recognized in this symbol, an evidence of the simplicity that had presided at the first graphic combinations of the Egyptians." (Lenormant, Researches on Horap., p. 26.)

Thebes was the city consecrated to Amon, the god of light, the divine word (Symbolic Colors, 70–71); the Hebrew name of Thebes is *Amon*, נא אמון; the manger was consecrated to Amon-Ra, the god-light, because the name of the manger was at the same time that of light.

אוֹרוּת AURUTH, or ארווֹת ARUUTH, a *manger*, a *stable*, is the feminine plural of אוֹרה, AURE, *light*, אוּר, AUR, the *sun, light, revelation*

CROCODILE.

Plutarch says that the crocodile was consecrated to Typhon. (Is. and Osir., cap. L.)

According to Diodorus of Sicily, this animal expressed in the hieroglyphics, all kinds of malice, of wickedness (III. 4, p. 176, Wessel's ed.).

Horapollo attributes the signification of rapacity, fury, to it (I. 67); it also designates the west (I. 69); the crocodile's tail was the symbol of darkness (I. 70); its eyes represented the east (I. 68).

The name of the crocodile appears to me to have been חמט, HEMT, a word translated in the Septuagint version by σαῦρα, and by the lexicographers, *lizard;* this name designates the entire *saurian* family, and, especially, the Egyptian crocodile. In Egypt, the same word designated the lizard and crocodile; for Horapollo says that the crocodile was the symbol of fecundity (I. 69), the idea represented on the monuments by the lizard. (Champ. Gramp., p. 347.)

The word חמט HEMT, *crocodile*, or *lizard*, is formed by the root חם HEM, *devouring heat*, חמה HEME, *incandescence, fury, poison*. The words formed by this root give the history of the myth of Typhon, genius of evil, symbolized, according to Plutarch, by the crocodile.

And, at first, we find the name of the ass also consecrated to Typhon ; חמור HEMUR, or חמר HEMR, the *ass*.

The name of the russet color attributed to Typhon (Symbolic Colors, 257) is חום HEUM, *black color*, *burnt color*; חמוץ HEMUTS, or חמץ HEMTS, the *red*, the *tawny*, the *oppressor*, the *violent* (see Art. *Russet Color*).

The word חמס HMS signifies *violence*, *injury*, *rapine*, and answers to the significations given to the crocodile by Horapollo, and to the Egyptian name of the animal

מסה MSH.[1]

The meaning here given to it by the Egyptian Hierogrammat and Hebrew homonymies, is confirmed by the monuments. One of the chapters in the Funereal Ritual relates to the combat between the deceased and the crocodile—that is, against his bad passions; he kills it · with the *Hoopoe* headed sceptre, the known emblem of virtuous affections.

In the Levitical, as in the Egyptian religion, the crocodile, חמט HEMT, is an unclean animal.

Horapollo adds that the crocodile was the symbol of fecundity (I. 69), and the word הם HEM presents the ideas of relationship, marriage; according to Gesenius, the Greek word *γάμος, marriage*, is derived from חם; we have just remarked that, on the monuments, the lizard was the symbol of fecundity.

According to Clement of Alexandria (Stromat. V. 7), the crocodile represented time; the Egyptian Saturn wore, as a head-piece, a crocodile's head, and the word חמק HEMQ, signifies *to make a circle*, *to turn around;* this word relates to the course of the sun, since חמה HEME signifies sun, and in Hebrew, the proper name of *time* signifies *to turn*, אפן APN, and forms אופן AUPN, a *wheel* (Gesenius).

According to Champollion, the lizard was consecrated to Bouto, divinity of primal darkness (Notice of the Museum Charles X., p. 42); according to Horapollo, the crocodile's tail was the symbol of darkness (I. 70), and the word חום HEUM signifies the *black color*, the color of darkness.

The name of Egypt, according to Plutarch (De. Is.

---

[1] In the Coptic we find again ⲙⲥⲁϩ *crocodilus*, ⲙⲥⲁϩ·ⲧⲉ *odie habere*.—EGYPT. GRAM., p. 384.

and Osir.), signified *blackness* and *heat;* חם HEM, *heat*, and חום HEUM, *blackness*, are a same root forming the name of the crocodile חמט HEMT; the name of Egypt preserved in the Bible is in fact חם HEM, and this word is inscribed on the obelisk at Paris by the *crocodile's tail* and the *nycticorax*, phonetically forming the word חם HEM.[1]

The signification of the name of Egypt is also found in the Coptic ⲔⲎⲙⲉ *black* (Champ. Gram., p. 320).

Why did the Egyptians give their country a reprobated name, composed of the Crocodile, symbol of darkness, and the Nycticorax, symbol of death (Horapol. I., 70, II., 25). The answer is clear; Egypt had three names; one, symbolized by the lily, designated Upper Egypt; the other, represented by the papyrus, Lower Egypt. These two names answer to the Hebrew words פתרוס PTHRUS, *Upper* Egypt, and מצור MTSUR, *Lower* Egypt; the first indicated the region of expounders and religion; the second, the land of agriculture and civilization, as explained under the article *lily* (consult the Art. *Vulture*).

The third name, חם HEM, or HAM, designated the profane, or dead men crouching in the darkness of ignorance *(Vide* Art. *Ass).*

Horus, the god of light, is sometimes represented under the form of a crocodile, with a hawk's head surmounted with horns, and the solar disk (Champ. Gram., p. 120). This confirms the assertion of Horapollo, that the crocodile's eyes represented light, and his tail darkness (I. 68, 70).

The Bible says: *The ancient and honorable, he is the head; and the prophet that teacheth lies, he is the tail.* (Isaiah ix., 15.)

FINGER.

" A finger designates the stomach of man" (Horap. II. 6). " This," says Lenormant, " is what we find in the Latin

---

[1] Salvolini, Trans. of Obelisk, p. 16. Akerblad, Letter to M. De Sacy, p. 37. Gesenius, verbo חם.

and French versions of Horapollo; but the Greek author was far from having so burlesque and inexplicable a thought; he simply made use of a Latin expression, not understood by his translators; στόμαχον, in Philippe's translation, means, as in Latin, *anger*. *The finger*, says he, *indicates the anger of man;* it is the *finger of God* in the scriptures. I think that the use of this sign is frequently found in the hieroglyphic texts; but I have not sufficient space to elaborate my opinion" (Lenormant, Research on Horap., p. 22).

The Hebrew word אצבע ATSBO, signifies a *finger*, and, metaphorically, *power, courage* (Guarin, Gesenius); הוא אצבע אלחים *there is the finger of God.*

WATER.

In Egyptian cosmogony, as in the first book of Moses, the world was created from the body of waters. This doctrine, says Champollion, was professed in Egypt in the most distant times (Pantheon Egyptien, Cnouphis-Nilus). Water was the *mother of the world*, the *matrix* of all created beings, and the word משבר MSCHBR signifies *matrix* and *waves*, משברים.

Man was considered as an image of the world, the initiate was to be born again to a new life, and the baptism thenceforward symbolized the primeval waters; it was on this account that the initiate was called משה MSCHE, *Moses*, a word signifying in Egyptian, according to Josephus (Antiq., II. 9, § 6), *saved from the water* or by the water, designated in Hebrew by משחה MSCHHEE, *unction* and משה MSCHE, *to save.*

In extending these philological researches, it would be easy to perceive that the word משבר, *matrix* and *wave*, is composed of that of the initiate משה and the name even of creation ברא BRA, *he created*, the first word of Genesis; moreover, בר BR signifies *a son, a child*, and *purity*, because the cosmogony became the symbol of spiritual birth or regeneration; according to Horapollo (I. 43), *water* was the symbol of *purity*, and designated the birth of the pure or initiates, as we shall show in the article *Dew*.

HAWK.

צ‎נ NTS, *the hawk*, forms the word נצה‎ NTSHE, *eternity, splendor*. According to Horapollo, this bird, on account of its long life, symbolized *divinity* as well as *the sun*, upon which he steadily gazed (Horap. I. 6). On the monuments the hawk is the sign of the idea *God* (Champ. Gram. Egypt, p. 118).

It represented *sublimity* and *humility*, adds the Egyptian philologist, because it flies in a straight line, up and down, נצה‎ NTSE, *to fly* (Gesenius).

It was the symbol of *blood*, because it drank no water, but blood; of *victory*, because it overcame all other birds (Horapol. I. 6, 7). נצה‎. NTSE, *to draw the sword, to devastate by war;* נצה‎ NTSHE (Chald.), *to vanquish*.

Horapollo further says that the hawk, spreading his wings in the air, represented the *wind*, as though the wind had wings (Horap. II. 15).

We discover from this passage that the hawk and wing, or the act of flying, were synonyms in the sacred language of Egypt; which we are also given to understand by Diodorus of Sicily, when he says that this bird represented everything done with celerity, because he surpassed all others in the rapidity of his flight (Diod. Sicul. III. 4, p. 145, ed. Rhodum).

צ‎נ NTS, *the hawk*, forms נצה‎ NTSE, *to fly*, נויה‎ NUTSE, *wing, feather*, נוץ‎ NUTS, *to fly, to fly away* (Gesenius). (Vide Essay on Hieroglyphics by M. Lacour, p. xxx.)

FACE.

M. Lepsius shows, in his letter to Rosellini (Annales, IX. 77 et seq.), that the name of the nose, in the sacred dialect, was 𓂺𓏤, a word of which no trace is to be found in the Coptic; its determinative is the figure of a calf's snout.

The nose and its name are employed in the sacred writings, with the signification of *residing in*.[1]

In the sacred tongue, the name of the nose, or, rather, that of the *face*, as proved by a variant, which we give here, according to the Egyptian grammar (p. 92), must, consequently, express the idea, *residing in*.

The Egyptian name ⳧𐦉𐦏, transcribed in Hebrew characters, gives the word פנתה PNTH, or PHNTH, the root of which we find again in the Hebrew word פנים PNIM, signifying *face, countenance*, facies, vultus, and at the same time what is *interior, within*, intus, intro (Rosenmüller) פנימי *the interior*, interior (Gesenius).

The name of the *nose* in Hebrew אף AP, comes, according to Gesenius, from אנף ANP, *the face, to respire by the nose*, a root which we likewise find in פנים PNIM, *face countenance*.

The different members of the *ox, bull*, or *calf* are used in the Egyptian grammar as determinatives, to denote those members in general; noticed by Champollion in his grammar, and Salvolini, Campagne de Rhamsès, 90. Is this the reason that the bull was the symbol of power (see Art. *Bull*). and that, consequently, the ear of that animal denoted *strength of hearing*, as the nose *the power of being within or of residing* ?

BEAN.

Herodotus relates that among the Egyptians the bean was considered an impure vegetable; the priests could not even bear the sight of it (Euterp. lib. II., cap. 37). The aversion of the Pythagorean disciples for this symbol of unclean things is also known.

The Hebrew explains this horror of the bean; the name of the vegetable is the same as that of the nomadic people, who were an abomination in the sight of the Egyptians.[2] In Genesis, Joseph says to his brethren:

---

[1] Lepsius, Annales, IX. 77 et seq.; Salvolini, Analysis, p. 229.

[2] The only difference is that bean is in the feminine, and nomadic people in the masculine gender.

2*

For every shepherd is an abomination unto the Egyptians (Gen. xlvi. 34).

גרה GRE, *the bean.*

גרים GRIM, *wandering shepherds.*

The name of the bean גרה GRE signifies *rumination,* and indicates that the vegetable was used in feeding the flocks.

As an expression of contempt, the wandering shepherds were called *bean-eaters,* because their existence depended on that of their flocks.

The bean gave its name to the wandering tribes, receiving from them the signification of impurity and abomination; which is again proved by the Hebrew, since גרה GRE, the *bean,* signifies, also, *to become furious, to make war.*

But how could the Hebrews, who were themselves a nomadic people, give a name characteristic of hatred and contempt to the wandering tribes? The difficulty can only be removed by supposing that the Hebrew tongue received its primitive form from a people who were not nomadic. The struggle between civilized people and the barbarous hordes is more strongly marked in the Irenian traditions than in those of Egypt.

FIG-TREE.

Horapollo says that the Egyptians represented a man cured of incontinence by a bull tied to a wild fig-tree, because the lascivious fury of the bull is appeased when he is tied to that tree (II. 77).

The bull was the symbol of fecundity and virile power, ἀνδρεῖον (Horap. I. 46). His Hebrew name, שר PR forms the verb פרה PRE, *to be fruitful* (See Art. *Bull*).

The name of the *fig-tree* תאנה THANE, further signifies *the conjugal act, coitum.*

The sign of the bull tied to that of the fig-tree represented man cured of incontinence; because, says Horapollo, in another chapter, the bull became continent by the act of incontinence itself; *Calidissimum enim est animal . . . . sed et temperans est, propterea quod numquam feminam ineat post conceptum* (I. 46).

Was it not the intention of the Egyptian priests thus to express that man, symbolized by the bull, only became continent when chained by marriage, represented by the fig-tree?

No Egyptian monument, at least none that I know of, represents a *bull tied to a fig-tree.* It is probable that this passage of Horapollo relates to a proverb or popular saying borrowed from the sacred tongue.

ANT.

The Egyptians represented *knowledge* or *intelligence*, γνῶσις, by the ant, because it finds what man hides with care; another reason, adds Horapollo, was, that, unlike other animals, when gathering provisions for winter, it never mistakes the place, but arrives there without error (Horap. I. 52).

The ant is here presented as a symbol of initiation, or of an initiate who has received knowledge, hidden by the priests from the vulgar.

The name of the ant, נמלה NMLE, is formed by the verb נמל NML, signifying *to circumcise.*

We learn from Herodotus (II. 36 and 104), Diodorus of Sicily (III. 32 in fine, Wessel, p. 198) and Philon (lib. Περὶ ἐπιτομῆς), that the initiates in the mysteries, who were instructed in the secret doctrines of the Egyptian priests, were circumcised; the cynocephalus, according to Horapollo, represented the priesthood, because it is naturally circumcised (Horap. I. 14. Leemans, Adnot. p. 204).

The Jewish people were initiated in the mysteries of true religion, and all Israelites had to be circumcised.

The fable of the Myrmidons, or ants changed into men, signifies that the profane who acquire *knowledge* of the mysteries, that the *circumcised*, or *ants*, become true men.

The particular relation between the ant and circumcision is, that the ant, according to the ancients, cut the top of the ear to get the grain out; to use the Hebrew expression, it *circumcised it* (Bochart, *Hierozoïcon*, II p. 5S7 et seq.; Job, c. xxiv. v. 24).

The symbolic signification given by Horapollo to the ant is consecrated by the proverbs of Solomon. *There be four things which are little upon the earth, but they are exceeding wise; the ants are a people not strong, yet they prepare their meat in the summer,* etc. (Proverbs xxx. 24.)

FROG.

The frog, according to Horapollo (I. 25), represents unformed man.

M. Champollion calls the frog *the emblem* of *primary matter, damp* and *without form ;*[1] the truth of this interpretation is demonstrated by the image of the Demiurgic Hercules, engraved on the base of a representation of that animal.[2]

This symbol is one of those that serve to identify iu the most unequivocal manner Egyptian Cosmogony and Initiation, since, on one hand, on the monuments deciphered by Champollion, the frog represents chaos, or primal matter, wet and without form, and, on the other, according to Horapollo, the frog is the symbol of *unformed man.*

That the world was born from the midst of the waters is taught by the Egyptiand octrines (see Article *Water*), as well as the first book of Moses ; thus the profane is compared to primal matter, damp and without form, over which the spirit has not yet moved, and which is born again from the waters of baptism (consult Symbolic Colors, p. 169).

The Hebrew name of the frog, צפרדע TSPRDO, is composed of צפר TSPR, *to turn, to convert one's self,* in a physical as in a moral sense ; this verb is applied to a timid and degraded man, who morally turns and returns on all sides (Gesenius). The second root of the name of the frog is דע DO, which signifies science, knowledge wisdom.

---

[1] Champollion, Notice du Musée Charles X., p. 40.
[2] Champ. ibid.

Thus the frog represents a man commencing to turn to wisdom ; it symbolizes the neophyte not yet spiritually formed, but who is about to be, or may become so. This symbol marks the undecided state of the mystes who may acquire a new life, or be replunged in darkness ; this is the meaning of Horapollo when he says in another chapter (II. 101), that the frog represents an *impudent* man, with a *brazen look ;* this animal also represents the profane combating wisdom. We find this second signification again in the Hebrew word, since צפר TSPR also signifies *to tear with nails* (claws), and דע DÓ, *wisdom ;* thus the frog is also the symbol of the shameless profane, who endeavors to destroy wisdom by false reasoning ; in this sense the Apocalypse speaks of *three unclean spirits like frogs* (xvi. 13), and that in Exodus, it is said that Aaron stretched out his hand over the waters of Egypt, and frogs came up and covered the land (Exodus viii., 1 to 10 ; Ps. lxxviii. 45.; cv. 30).

The Egyptian philologist adds further on (II. 102), that man, who had remained a long time without motion, and who was subsequently enabled to move, was symbolized by a frog having its hind legs, because the frog comes into the world without them.

The motionless man, having acquired the power of motion, is also the regenerated man, for in Hebrew שוה SCHUHE signifies to *walk,* and to *meditate* (Rosen müller), and הלך ELK to *walk,* and *to live ;* הלך תמים *he who walks uprightly* (Ps. xv. 2).

AXE.

This sign, which certainly represents an axe, as explained by Champollion in his Grammar, p. 5 and 110, and, as proved by Wilkinson's description of Egypt, (*Manners of the Egyptians,* I. 323), is the sign of the idea *God.*

His name in Egyptian is composed of the axe, the segment of a sphere, and the mouth ; which gives, in accordance with Champollion's alphabet, the word גדר NDR, which signifies in Hebrew a *vow*, a *thing vowed*, *consecrated*. These different acceptations are applied to the consecrated images of the gods, and to the temples.

The root of this name of *consecration* גדר NDR is גדה NDE, to *separate*, because things vowed or consecrated were set apart ; the axe was the sign of the idea to separate, and the word גדה NDHE especially signified to strike with the axe (Deut. xx. 19, Gesenius[1]).

Salvolini seeks an explanation of this symbol in the word ךεp (Analysis, p. 230) ; I will only call attention to the fact, that our group, according to Lepsius, forms the word Xοϒϒεp (Annales, ix. 77, 81), which also appears in the Hebrew גדר.

SWALLOW.

In Egypt, the swallow was the symbol of *the entire heritage left to children ;* because, says Horapollo, when about to die, it rolls itself in the mud and forms a nest for its young (Horap. II., 31).

The Hebrew name of the *swallow* is דרור DRUR ; the root of this word is דר DR or דור DUR, words having alike the signification :

1. *Habitation, house*, which answers to the word in Horapollo κτῆσιν, *possession*, which I translate by inheritance.

2. דור DUR also signifies a *generation*, γενεά (seventy), and consequently answers to Horapollo's words κτῆσιν γονικήν, *generative possession*, or paternal inheritance.

The swallow was the symbol of ancestral inheritance, because it built its nest in the habitation of man ; on which account it was consecrated to the household gods (Noël).

---

[1] The name of the Nazarites גזיר signifies *consecrated* and *separated* גזר *separavit se, abstinuit, se consecravit* (Gesenius).

EIGHT.

"The god Thoth," says Salvolini, "was regarded in ancient Egypt as the protector of the city of Hermopolis Magna; on this account, he everywhere receives in the inscriptions the title which is found in the character ⲚⲎⲂ *lord*, followed by the number *eight*. That the reader may understand the origin of the use of the number eight in the expression of this divine title, it will only be necessary for me to remind him that the Egyptian name of *Hermopolis* reads ϢⲘⲞⲨⲚ SCHMOUN, and that in the Coptic as well as in the Egyptian, a word identical with this name ϣⲙⲟⲩⲛ indicates the number *eight*." (Analysis, p. 230.)

In Hebrew, also, the word *eight* is שמנה SCHMNE.

KNOTTED CORDS.

Horapollo says in a passage, altered by the copyists, that *knotted cords*, *παγὶς*, represented in the hieroglyphics *love*, *the chase*, *death*, *the air* and *a son*. (Horap., lib. II., 26. *Vide* Leemans, Adnot.) I do not attempt to reproduce the text, I only give the words it contains and which I also find in the significations or the root of the Hebrew name of *knotted cords*.

SIGNIFICATIONS GIVEN BY HORAPOLLO.	SIGNIFICATIONS OF THE NAME OF KNOTTED CORDS IN HEBREW.
Knotted cords	חבל HEBL, knotted cords.
The chase	חבל HEBL, knotted cords, nets.
A son	חבל HEBL, childbirth, a child.
Death	חבל HEBL (Chald.), to destroy, corruption.
The air	הבל EBL, the breeze.
Love	חבב HEBB, to love.

HARE.

The Egyptians represented the idea of an *opening*, ἄνοιξις, by the *hare*, because this animal always has its eyes open (Horap. I. 26.) ; the monuments confirm this signification *to open* or an *opening* (Leemans, p. 235).

According to Champollion, the hare was the symbol of Osiris (Notice Musée Charles X., p. 46) ; that divinity being represented by the *eye*, and the hare designating *open eyes*.

The Hebrew gives the reason of this use of the symbol, since ארנבת ARNBTH, the *hare*, is composed of אר AR, *light*, and נבב NBT, *to contemplate, to have intuition*.[1]

The word ארבה ARBE, an *opening*, an *open window*, is composed of the same roots as the name of the hare.[2]

According to the Hebrew signification of the name of this animal, it should be in Egypt the symbol of moral light revealed to the neophytes, and contemplation of divinity, which explains why it was the symbol of Osiris.

LION.

Horapollo says that the Egyptians represented the *soul* or *incandescence* θυμὸς, by the lion (Horap. I. 17).

The Hebrew name of the lion לביא LBIA, is formed of the root לב LB, signifying *soul, heart* ; לבה LBE, *flame, heart*.

Horapollo adds, that the lion is remarkable for the size

[1] The last letter is here changed from ה to ב because in Hebrew these two letters are thus often changed (Gesen., p. 383) ; be that as it may, there can be no doubt as to the root, since it comes from the verb נבב, to pierce, to open, which forms the words נבא *to prophecy*, and נבט *to contemplate*.

[2] אר, *light*, and בבה or נבבה an *opening, a door*, of נבב *to pierce, to open* (Gesenius *verbo* בבב).

of his head, his flaming eyes, his face surrounded with a radiating mane like the sun, and that it is on this account that lions are placed under the throne of Horus, to show the symbolical relations between this animal and divinity.

The name of Horus, the god Sun, signifies, likewise, in Hebrew the sun, אור AUR, pronounced HOR or אר, AR, the *sun*.

ארי ARI is one of the Hebrew names of *lion* and of *fire;* the word אריאל ARIAL is interpreted by *lion of God* or *fire of God* and אראל ARAL, *lion of God, heroes* (Gesenius).

Thus, according to Horapollo, the symbolic relations existing between the god Sun and the lion are clearly manifested in the Hebrew.

The *hinder parts of the lion*, according to the same author, had the signification of strength (Horap. I. 18). The word ליש LISCH designates a *lion* and *strength* (Gesenius).

The head of the lion, says Horapollo, was the symbol of vigilance and care, because that animal closes his eyes when waking and opens them when asleep, which designates vigilance : it was on account of this symbolic quality that lions were placed as guardians at the inclosures of the temples (Horap. I. 19).

The lion's head was particularly chosen to designate care and vigilance, on account of the relations established between the lion and the sun; the name of Horus or light אר AR forms the verb ראה RAE *to see, to foresee, to contemplate;* and the name of the lion ארי ARI forms that of *vision* ראי RAI.

According to Champollion, the lion was the emblem of Phtha and of Aroeris (Notice Musée Charles X., p. 43).

In the Coptic we find ⲙⲟⲩⲓ *lion*, and ⲟⲩⲉ *splendor.*

LILY OR LOTUS.

A lily-stalk, or a bunch of the same plant, expressed the idea of the region of Upper Egypt; a stalk of the papyrus with its tuft, or a bouquet of the same plant was the symbol of Lower Egypt (Champ. Egypt. Gram., p. 25 ; Rosetta Inscription, line 5).

The lily or lotus symbolized initiation or the birth of celestial light; on some monuments the god Phre (the sun) is represented as coming forth from the cup of a lotus (Champ. Musée Charles X, p. 18 : Jablonski, *Horus*, p. 212).

The Hebrew name of Upper Egypt פתרוס PTHRUS is formed from the root פתר PTHR, *to interpret dreams.*

Upper Egypt was the native country of auguries, the cradle of religion, of initiation, and science, as the lotus was the cradle of Phre, the *sun.*

The papyrus, the sign on the Rosetta-stone of Lower Egypt, indicated, says Horapollo, the *first food of man* and *the earliest origin of things* (Horap. I. 30).

The Hebrew name of Lower Egypt is מצור MTSUR, formed from the roots מצה MTSE, *unleavened bread, first food of man,*[1] and of צור TSUR, *to gather together, to tie together,* צרר TSRR, a truss; the truss of papyrus was, according to Horapollo, the symbol of *the early origin of things.*

Following the Hebrew significations, Lower Egypt was the land of agriculture and the gathering of men in society, which is indicated by its name מצור, *Egypt* and a *frontier*, a *citadel*, a *fortified city*, and which is also expressed in the hieroglyphics by *bread*, מצה MTSE, root of the name of Lower Egypt (see Art. *Sacred Bread*).

Egypt had a third name, explained in the Article *Crocodile.*

MOON.

The Egyptians represented the *month* by a *moon* or by a *palm-branch* (Horap. I. 4).

In Hebrew the name of the month and that of the moon form a single word ירח IRHE, *moon* and *month;* as in the Coptic ⲟⲟϩ., *moon* and *month.*

---

[1] The papyrus was the earliest food of the Egyptians (Herodotus, II. 92).

The palm does not designate a month, but a year, as proved by the monuments (Egypt. Gram., p. 97), and as established by Horapollo himself in another passage (I. 3).

The Hebrew name of the palm, or palm-branch, is סנסנה SNSNE, *ramus palmæ;* the root of this word is found again in שנה SCHNE, the *year*.[1]

HAND.

Horapollo says that the Egyptians represented a man fond of building by a hand, because from the hand proceed all labors (II. 119).

יד ID, *hand*, signifies also a *monument*, and *force, power, vigor*.

Hands joined were the symbol of concord (Horap. II. 11).

In Hebrew שלח SCHLHE, *to give the hand*, forms the word שלום SCHLUM, *concord* (Gesenius).

SHE-MULE.

The she-mule, says Horapollo, represents a barren woman (II. 42).

The word פרד PRD, a *mule*, signifies also to *separate*, to *disjoin*, a verb applicable to the separation of the sexes.

EGYPTIAN GOOSE.

The Egyptians, says Horapollo, represented the idea of *son* by the chenalopex goose. This animal exhibits

---

[1] According to Gesenius, the letters ש and ס are interchangeable in Hebrew. He even gives examples in the root סנה.

great tenderness for its little ones—the father and mother precipitating themselves, in defense, against the hunters who endeavor to take them (Horap. I. 53).

The Egyptian monuments confirm this interpretation (Champollion, Précis, p. 119, 218; Leemans on Horap., p. 276).

The Abydos tablet has ten repetitions of a group composed of the goose and solar disk above the royal cartouches;[1] Champollion translates this group by son of the sun (Précis., p. 218).

The word *son* in Hebrew is בר BR; this word twice repeated with the plural indication, signifies *geese*, ברברים BRBRIM (Gesenius).

EAR.

According to Horapollo, the ear of a bull represented *hearing* (I. 47).

This sign is the determinative of the verbs *to hear*, *to listen* (Champ. Gram., 387, 388).

The word אזן AZN signifies an *ear*, *to hear*, *to listen*, and also *to be sharp*, whence, says Gesenius, comes the name of ear, because *among animals* that organ *is sharp*. This remark is the commentary on the passage from Horapollo and the hieroglyphic representing the ear.

The bull's ear also symbolized a *future thing* or a *future fact* (Horap. II. 23), because it was the symbol of *hearing*, and, in the sacred language, the name *hearing* signified a *future thing*, as appears in the Hebrew, since שמע SCHMO signifies to *hear*, to *listen*, to *announce*, to *call up* (Gesenius; consult Champ. Gram., 387). See Article *Goat*.

In a manuscript in the royal library, is a personage having his head surmounted by two bull's ears, and

---

[1] Vide *Klaproth*, Observation on the Monument of Abydos, following an Examination of Champollion's labors; *Leemans*, on Horapollo, page 276; *Salt*, Essay on Phonetic Hieroglyphics.

reading a book on which is the name of Osiris. (This is the vignette to our fourth chapter.)

He that hath ears to hear, let him hear! Ὁ ἔχων ὦτα ἀκούειν, ἀκουέτω! (Luke viii. 8). These words of Jesus Christ spoken after a parable, signify that he who hears the recital of similitudes, should endeavor to discover their hidden meaning and be obedient to their teaching, for the Hebrew name of hearing signifies to *understand* and *obey*. שמע SCHMO, *audivit, audita intellexit, intellectus est, obedivit* (Gesenius).

QUAIL BONE.

A *quail bone*, says Horapollo, expresses *stability* and *safety* (II. 10).

The word עצם, OTSM, signifies at once *bone* and *solidity, strength*. (*Os* a firmitate et robore dictum, *Gesenius*.)

The name of the quail, שלו, *schlu*, is the same word as שלי, *schlu*, which expresses *stability* and *safety* (*securus, securitas*. Gesenii Lexicon Manuale. p. 964 et 1007).[1]

This Egyptian symbol is, likewise, a trope of Bible symbology; when the Psalmist says: *There is no security in my bones because of my sins* (Ps. xxxviii. 3). He employs the word שלים SCHLUM, of which the root, שלי, also indicates *security* and *quail*, and the word עצם, OTSM, which designates a *bone* and *firmness, solidity*.

---

[1] I again call the attention of the reader, who is but slightly acquainted with the Hebrew language, to the fact, that I entirely neglect the vowel-points. This principle, which I apply to the Hebrew because there are no vowel-points in Egyptian, is followed by Hebraists in interpreting significant names; that of the quail is in point; it was thus named, say the Commentators, because it lives in *security* in the midst of the harvest (Robertson, *Thesaurus Linguæ Sanctæ*).

In applying this rule, a single letter might prove embarrassing. The letter ש forms two series in the dictionaries, according to the place occupied by the point, שׁ and שׂ. This letter being doubled, it will be understood that in the other series the words in which it appears differently pointed cannot be found side by side; thus the name of the *quail* שלו is found on page 964 of Gesenius' Lexicon, and its homonym שלו appears on page 1007. In like manner the word משוקק is n)t placed beside משה, etc., etc.

SHE-BEAR.

The Egyptians, says Horapollo, wishing to designate a child unshapen at birth, and afterwards formed, paint a bear with young, because she brings forth condensed blood, which she transforms by warming it on her breast, and which she finishes by licking (Horap. II. 83).

This symbol would be unintelligible without the explanation to be found in Hebrew.

The name of the constellation, *great bear*, עש, OSCH, forms the obsolete word עשה, OSCHE, which, according to Gesenius, must have signified *the hairy, he who is covered with hair like a bear.*

The same word, עשה, OSCHE, signifies *to form, to manufacture, to create*, an expression employed in Genesis in speaking of the creation of the world.

This child, unshapen at its birth, warmed on the maternal breast, and perfected by caresses, is the world, which in chaos was without form, and was finished by the love of God.

The child unshapen at its birth is likewise an emblem of the soul, which from the state of the profane rises, by regeneration, to a moral and spiritual state. I have often said, and I repeat it, the initiation was the type of cosmogony; regeneration, or spiritual creation of man, was presented as an image of the creation of the world (Symbolic Colors, p. 96. See Article *Beetle* hereafter).

CONSECRATED BREAD.

Many geographical proper names, says Champollion (Egypt. Gram., p. 151), have the *consecrated bread* for determinatives; the Egyptians, adds that learned man, desired, apparently, to express, by such a determinative, countries or localities inhabited and organized in regular societies.

Salvolini, in acknowledging the general signification

of this sign, pretends that it only applied to Egypt ; according to this philologist, no form of bread on the monuments refers to the sign as we explain it ; he has it that it is the figurative sign of the horizon (Translation of the Obelisk, p. 16 and 17).

Salvolini was in too much haste in denying the fact advanced by his master. Several monuments in the Egyptian Museum at Paris prove that our sign is consecrated bread ; the chest No. 3293 represents an offering of variously shaped bread: our sign, as we give it, and as it is found in Champollion's Grammar and Salvolini's alphabet, appears there several times.

Besides, the Hebrew clears up the difficulty, since the word כבר, KKR, signifies *bread*, a *cake*, a *country*, a *region*.

Again, מצה, MTSE, *unleavened bread*, forms the word מצור, MTSUR, which signifies *Egypt*, and a *frontier*.

PAPYRUS.

Horapollo says, that the highest antiquity was represented by *discourses* (writings ?), *leaves*, or a *sealed book* (II. 27).

Now, the word עלה, OLE, which signifies a *leaf*, and *to inscribe on tablets*, forms עלם, OLM, and עילם, OULM, the *antique origin of things, obscure time, hidden, eternity*.[1]

The papyrus-leaf, that plant which formed tablets and books, is the first letter of the name of the only eternal and all-powerful god of Egypt, *Amon*, who in the beginning of things created the world. The name of the god *Amon*, according to Manetho cited by Plutarch, signified *occult*, or *hidden*. The first letter of the name of Egyptian gods is often symbolic, since this initial forms, in many cases, the special attribute of the divinity.

The fasces and the papyrus-leaf were specially chosen

---

[1] From whence also the name of *nursling*, and the verb *to nurse*, עול OUL. Milk is a child's first nourishment, as the papyrus was the earliest food of the Egyptians (Herodotus II. 92).

to represent obscure and hidden antiquity, and the name of the *papyrus*, אבה, ABE, appears to belong to the same root as הבא, HEBA, *to hide, to hide one's self.*

We may here assign the reason why the bunch of papyrus is the determinative of female names : according to cosmogony, love was the first origin of things : אהב AEB, *love,* and אבה ABE, *the papyrus,* evidently belong to the same root.[1]   Again, עלם OLM, *the antique origin of things,* signifies a young man at puberty ; עלמה OLME, *a marriageable girl.*   These words come from the root עלה OLE, a *leaf* (consult Articles, *Bunch of Reed, Lily,* and that on the color *Green*).

EYELIDS.

Champollion supposes the three upper signs to represent *diadems* (Gram., p. 298, 440) ; but this supposition is not confirmed by any form of diadem.

Salvolini thinks these signs are *crests* (Alphabet, No. 194).

I think I recognize *eyelids;* in fact, these three signs are covered with a sort of eyelid or brow showing itself above the eyes, the design of which is given by Champollion (Egypt. Gram., consult Nos. 208 and 242, of Alphabet).

This sign, according to Champollion, marks the idea of *festival* (Gram., p. 174).

The Hebrew name of *eyelid* is the same as that of the celebration of a *festival.*

שמרה SCHMRE, in the feminine plural שמרות SCHMRUTH, *eyelids ;* and in the plural masculine שמרים SCHMRIM, *observatio, celebratio festi* (Gesenius).

---

[1] The common root of these two words is אב, *father, Creator, will, verdure, grass, a fruit.*   All these significations were connected together in the cosmogony : the Creator, God, formed the world in his love or his will ; the grass, verdure, the leaves, represented the birth of the world, because nature seems to be born again when the leaves appear

The eyelid was the symbol of observation or the celebration of a feast, because the name of the eyelid in Hebrew signified *vigilance* and *watchfulness*, שמרה SCHMRE, *custodia*. In Egypt, the lion's head was the symbol of *vigilance;* because, says Horapollo, that animal closes his eyes when waking and opens them in sleeping (*Vide* Art. *Lion*). On the monuments, the lion's head has the signification of *vigilance*. Does not the sign we are considering represent the lion's eyelid, symbol of vigilance, of watchfulness, or of the observation of religious feasts?

PEDUM OR DIVINING ROD.

" In each step of the hieroglyphics," says Salvolini, ' we meet with the idea of a king, or, to speak more correctly, of a *moderator*, expressed by the *ΥΚ* spoken of by Manetho ; it is always written as follows :

ᴅ⌒ ᕃκ, ᕃικ. The image of an individual clothed with all the emblems of royalty, the *ureus* on his forehead, the *pedum* and the *whip* between his knees, serving as a determinative. The *pedum*, symbol of moderation, by a process peculiar to Egyptian writings, serves also to express the initial of the word ᕃικ , *moderator*" (Campagne de Rhamsès, p. 16).

The transcription of the above group gives the Hebrew word חק HEQ, which signifies a *law*, a *statute*, a *custom;* חקק HEQQ, a *legislator*, a *chief*, and a *sceptre* (Gesenius), or a *king moderator* and a *pedum*.

3

OSTRICH FEATHER.

The ostrich feather is a symbol frequently used in hieroglyphic writing and anaglyphs, its signification of *justice* and *truth* being well established.[1]

According to Horapollo, " The man rendering *justice* to all, was represented by the ostrich feather; because that bird, unlike others, has all its feathers equal" (Horap., II. 118).

The ostrich feather is the symbol of the goddess of justice and truth, *Thme*, the Egyptian Themis.

The Hebrew word יען ION, signifies an *ostrich* and a *council*, a *determination*. This word comes, according to Gesenius, from the root ענה ONE, *to declare a sentence*, and at the same time *to testify* (Gesenius, p. 780, B). Thus in Hebrew as in Egyptian, the ostrich is the symbol of a *sentence of justice*, and of a *testimony of truth;* let us add that the name of the goddess of *justice* and *truth*, *Thme*, signifies in Hebrew *justice* and *truth*, תם THM or תמה THME, *integritas* and *ἀλήθεια*.

Poetically, the Hebrew name of the *ostrich* is רננה RNNE ; this word also signifies *a song of joy*, *of praise*, and, according to Champollion, happy souls, their heads ornamented with the *ostrich feather*, and under the inspection of the lord of the *heart's joy*, gathered fruits from celestial trees (Letters from Egypt, p. 231).

A painting of the Funeral Ritual represents the judgment of a soul; it advances toward the goddess *Thme*, who wears an ostrich feather on her head; beside this divinity of justice and truth, appears the scale in which *Anubis* and *Horus* weigh the actions of the deceased—they place in one side the ostrich feather, and in the

---

[1] There can be no doubt as to the sign representing an ostrich feather, since, in a painting of Thebes, we see two men occupied in pulling feathers from an ostrich (*Wilkinson's* Manners and Customs of the Ancient Egyptians, II. 6).

other the vase containing the heart;[1] if the weight of the heart is greater than that of the ostrich feather, the scale descends, and the soul is received in the celestial courts; above this scene appear the forty-two judges of the souls seated, and having the head ornamented with the ostrich feather.[2]

FISH.

The *fish*, according to Horapollo (I. 44), was a symbol of evil omen, designating *crime μῦσος*.

In Hebrew, דג DG, *fish*, forms the verb דגה DGE, *to cover, to hide, to be in darkness*. In Egypt, darkness was the symbol of Typhon, personification of crime, hatred, and every ill. Another name of the fish דאג DAG, forms the word דאגה DAGE, *fear, solicitude*.

HOG.

The Egyptians represented an unclean man by a *hog* (Horap. II. 37).

The sow was the emblem of Thoueris and other typhonian goddesses (Champ. Notice Musée Charles X., 48).

Like the Egyptians, the Israelites regarded swine as unclean.

The word הזיר HEZIR, a *hog*, is formed by the verb זיר ZIR, *to be disgusted*.

---

[1] Horap., I. 21 : Leemans, Adnot. and plate XLV, A. See the last vignette at the end of the volume, copied from the manuscript of Tentamoun.

[2] See Explanation of the principal painted scene of the Egyptian funeral papyrus by Champollion the younger, from the *Bulletin universal des Sciences*, by Férussac, Nov., 1825. Consult Notice Musée Charles X. ; Description of Egypt, etc.

RAT.

The rat, according to Horapollo, was the symbol of *destruction* (Horap. I. 50).

The root of the Hebrew word פרה PRE, a *rat* (Gesenius), is פרר PRR, *to break, to destroy*.

The word עכבר OKBR is also the name of the rat; it is composed, according to Gesenius, of עכל OKL, to *consume*, and בר BR, *wheat*. Several loaves being placed together, says Horapollo, the rat chooses and eats the best.

The rat was again, according to the same author, the sign of the idea of *judgment*, because he chose the best part of the bread. The name of the *rat*, פרה PRE, forms the word פרז PRZ, a *judge, he who separates, divides* (pr. *dirimens, judex,* Gesenius).

The vignette at the head of this chapter, copied from the Tentamoun manuscript, exhibited in the Royal Library, represents the *judgment* of the soul; the defunct, assisted by a personage with a *rat's head*, presents in his hands the works done and the words spoken during life and according to which he is to be judged.[1]

REED.

This sign represents a reed, or, as Salvolini has it, a *graminous plant* (Alp., No. 144).

The words *govern* and *direct* have this sign frequently given them as an initial instead of its homophones (Egypt. Gram., 74); it likewise forms the first letter of the word *king* (Ibid. p. 75; Abydos Tablet).

---

[1] *The eye* signifies *to do*, p. 15; and the *mouth* is the symbol of speech. See "Origin of the Egyptian Language," by Dr. Lowe, p. 21

Plutarch, in a passage altered from the treatise on Isis and Osiris (cap. XXXVI), and restored by the commentators (*vide* Leemans, Adnot. ad Horap., p. 292), says that the *reed* was the symbol of *royalty*, of *irrigation*, and the *fecundation of all things*

The Hebrew word שדה SCHDE signifies a *field, region, possession, royalty, woman;* it must also have had, according to Gesenius (p. 983), the signification *to sprinkle*, and, according to Guarin, that of *grass*.

שדי SCHDI designates a *field* and the *All-powerful*.[1]

The various acceptations of these words come from their root שד SCHD, signifying a *teat*, sign of the *fecundation of all things*.

The Egyptian inscriptions confirm this application of the Hebrew.

On the Abydos tablet, the word *king* is always written by the *reed* and the *segment of a sphere*, which according to Champollion's alphabet gives the word שד SCHD, root of the Hebrew words we have just examined. The word *king* is also often written coupled with the sign of *water* or the crown (Egypt. Gram., p. 75), which gives the word שדן SCHDN.

But Lepsius demonstrates that the final N is only a derivative augmentation not belonging to the primitive word (Annales de l'Institut de correspondance archéologique, tome X, p. 121, 122). This word is not in the Coptic, though Lepsius thinks he discovers a trace of it in the name of the *Basilisk* ⲥⲓⲧ, symbol of the Egyptian kings (Ibid. p. 122).

DEW.

The Egyptians represented teaching or instruction, παιδεία, by the dew falling from heaven (Horap. I. 37).

---

[1] שורי *campus, ager ;* שדי *potentissimus, omnipotens.* See שדה and שדה.

In Hebrew ירה IRE signifies *to throw drops of water, to sprinkle* and *to teach, to instruct* (Gesenius).

In like manner, מורה MURE, signifies *a doctor, a professor*, and the *first rain*, which, in Palestine, falls from the middle of October to the middle of December and prepares the earth to receive the seed (Gesenius, verbo יורה).

The symbolic relation between *instruction*, which prepares man for intellectual life, and the *first rain*, which prepares the germination of plants, will be understood.

The word מלקוש MLQUSCH designates spring rain, which in Palestine falls before harvest, in the months of March and April ; Job assimilates this rain to speech full of eloquence and good fruits (Job. xxix. 23.)

The sign we give here, is an abridgment of the scene representing Egyptian baptism, or shedding celestial dew on the head of the neophyte.

The vignette in the beginning of this work shows the baptism, after a design of the *Monuments of Egypt and Nubia by Champollion* (tome I. pl. XLII).

Horus and Thoth-Lunus pour water on the head of the neophyte, which is transformed to *divine life* (ansated cross) and to *purity* (Hoopoe headed sceptre[1]).

The legend accompanying this scene, and of which all the elements are known, should, I think, be thus translated : *Horus, son of Isis, baptizes with water and fire (repeat), Horus baptizes with water and fire (repeat): to be pronounced four times.*

The same legend is repeated for Thoth-Lunus, with the change of name only.

From this monument we learn the words spoken by the priests during the ceremony.   He who represented Horus, *twice* said : Horus, son of Isis, baptizes with water and fire, then *twice:* Horus baptizes with water and fire ; he repeated these same words *four times.*

Thoth-Lunus pronounced the same phrases the same number of times, substituting his titles for those of Horus.

---

[1] The signification of the ansated cross is recognized by all Egyptologists ; as to that of the Hoopoe Sceptre, Champollion gives it a different meaning from that of Horapollo, that of *purity*, instead of *piety* (Egyptian Gram., p. 290, 412, 449, or *pure*, 90).   We have seen that *water* was the symbol of *purity*.

Thus the words *baptism of fire and water* were repeated SIXTEEN times by each initiator; altogether THIRTY-TWO times. These numbers had a signification which Horapollo has preserved for us: *sixteen* symbolized pleasure, love; and *twice sixteen* marriage or conjunction, resulting from reciprocal love. It would be difficult not to see that it is a question here of the marriage of the two principles represented by the sun and moon, or *Horus* and *Thoth-Lunus*, of which we shall speak in our last article.[1]

The baptism of water and fire, designated in the legend by the character ⟨symbol⟩ that Leemans has explained in his annotations on Horapollo (p. 261, and plate XLIX), is identical in its exterior form with *the baptism of water, the Spirit, and of fire*, in the Bible (Luke iii., 16, 17). We likewise find the baptism of fire and Spirit in the sign of the dew, copied in Champollion's alphabet (Egypt. Gram.) and which represents three series of triangles or pyramids, symbols of fire and light.[2]

The name received by the *baptized* or *anointed* was that given in the Bible to the chief of the Hebrews, *Moses*, משה; this name exists on the Egyptian monuments, it is written by the sign of the *dew* or *baptism*, equal to מ, and the bent stalk equal to ש; the group ⟨symbol⟩ in Hebrew מש or משה is translated in Champollion's Grammar by *begotten* (p. 133); we give it the signification of *regenerated* or *begotten again*, with reference to the long series of proper names, among which are the names of the gods followed by this group. Thus *Thoutmos, Amenmos, Harmos, Phtahmos* designated the regenerated by *Thoth, Amon, Horus* or *Phtah*.

According to the Bible, the name of Moses was Egyp-

---

[1] *Vide* Horap. I. 33. See, for meaning of the word we translate by *baptize*, Egypt. Gram., p. 376 and 360; and for that of the group which we read *repeat*, see Champolliou, Letters from Egypt and Nubia, p. 196 and 146, pl. VI.

[2] Consult a monument in Champollion's Egyptian Pantheon (Plate XV, A), where these triangles are painted red and yellow, colors consecrated to fire and light. See, also, a note of Leemans on Horapollo, p. 248.

tian, and signified *saved by water* or *from the water*.
שמי משה והאמר כי מן־המים משיתחו ותקרא (Exodus ii., 10).

In Hebrew Moses, משה MSCHE, signifies *saved*, and משה
MSCHHE is the verb *to anoint* and *consecrate;* thus the
Egyptian name given to Moses, designates one saved by
unction or *baptism.* He received this baptism in infancy
and manhood, since, according to the Acts of the Apostles and Philo, he was learned in all the wisdom of the
Egyptians.[1]

SACK OF WHEAT.

. **/** . **(**

This sign represents an empty *wheat sack*, as proved
by a monument engraved in Rosellini's work. Champollion thought it was a kind of purse (Egypt. Gram.,
p. 55).

The Hebrew word תבואה THBUAE, signifies *the revenue
of the land*, the *product of the fields*, and also the *fruit of
intelligence* (Gesenius).

The word תבון THBUN, belonging to the same root,
designates *intelligence, prudence.*

A chief, or leading personage in a hierarchy, was
represented in Egypt by the figure of a man standing,
with a pure sceptre in one hand and the sack of wheat
in the other (Champ. Egypt. Gram., p. 55).

The sceptre was the symbol of power,[2] and the sack
of wheat the emblem of *intelligence, of prudence*, and the
right of proprietor in lands.

Mercury, the god of material and intellectual riches,
held a purse in his hand like the Egyptian chiefs.

---

[1] Acts vii. 22. Philon, de vita Mosis, lib. I. p. 606. See Lowe
The origin of the Egyptian language, p. 26–27 ; and Lacour's Essay
on Hieroglyphics.

[2] The *pure sceptre*, or staff without ornament שבט, represented the
instrument with which the guilty were stricken, and the scourge of God.
The pure sceptre was, consequently, the sign of the right to punish and
of the power of chiefs.

BEETLE.

In Egypt, the beetle was the symbol of *creation by a single power,* μονογενὲς, of *generation,* of *paternity,* the *world* and *man* (Horap. I. 10).

" The beetle," adds Horapollo, "represented procreation by a single individual, because that insect has no female ; when it wishes to procreate it forms a ball, image of the world, of ox dung, which it rolls with its hinder parts from east to west, looking to the east ; it buries this ball in the earth for twenty-eight days, and on the twenty-ninth throws it into the water."

The Hebrew name of the beetle is צלצל TSLTSL, which Gesenius translates cricket (*bestiola stridens, grillus*).

When this insect wishes to beget, it walks backward towards the region of darkness, the west ; and the Hebrew name of the beetle is formed of צל TSL, *shadow, darkness,* צלל TSLL, *to obscure, to overshadow.*

It rolls, the image of the world, the ball, with its posterior claws, and the same word צלל TSLL signifies to *roll underneath* (Gesenius).

It buries this ball in the earth, and afterwards throws it into the water ; the same word צלל TSLL signifies to *cover* and to *submerge* (Rosenmüller, Vocab.), from whence is formed צולה TSULE, *the depths of the sea* (Gesenius).

This symbol represents the drama of initiation ; the ball of excrement from whence is to come forth the new beetle, is the image of our body of corruption—buried in the earth it dies and is born again to a new life, being fructified by the baptismal waters. The initiation symbolized death and a new birth (Symbolic Colors, p. 168, et seq.).

The beetle was the symbol of the *world* and of *man,* because, in the doctrine of the mysteries, man was the little world, and the world, the great man (Symb. Col., p. 184). In the Egyptian grammar the beetle designated the *terrestrial world* (Champ. Gram., p. 377) ; and on mummy-cases the beetle with spread wings, rolling the globe,

3*

doubtless represented the death and new birth of the
celestial neophyte.

Man is μονογενὲς, that is to say, regenerated by God
alone. God, who warms the heart and enlightens the
mind, was symbolized by the sun; and from Clement
Alexandrinus (Stromat V.), as well as Horapollo (I. 10),
we learn that the beetle symbolized the sun: the god
Thra, one of the forms of *Phre* (the sun), has a beetle
in place of a head.

The fathers of the church adopted these Egyptian
symbols, preserved by the priests, when they named
Jesus the μονογενὲς, and the *good beetle*. St. Ambrosius
seems to translate Horapollo when he says: *Et bonus
scarabæus, qui lutum corporis nostri ante informe ac pigrum
virtutum versabat vestigiis : bonus scarabæus, qui de stercore
erigit pauperem* (St. Amb. in Luke X., No. 113. See
also Leemans, Adnot. ad Horap., p. 162).

SIGNET.

The signet is the determinative of the verbs *to close,
to shut, to seal* (Champ. Gram., p. 372).

In Hebrew חתם HETHM, a *signet*, a *seal ring*, and the
same word signifies *to close, to shut, to seal*, and likewise
to accomplish, to finish (Gesenius).

The Egyptian word given by Champollion is

ϣⲧⲩ, ⲃⲧⲩ, which is the pronunciation of

the Hebrew word חתם HETHM.

The Coptic word ϣⲧⲁⲙ certainly signifies *to shut,
to close*, but in no wise designates a *signet*. The only
Coptic name of the *signet*, given in Peyron's dictionary,
belongs to the root of the word *finger*, ⲧⲉⲃ , which
forms the verbs *to sign with a seal, to confirm*, and the
name of the *signet ring*, but does not express the ideas
to close, to shut.

SPHINX.

The symbolic signification of the sphinx is found in Hebrew: צפן TSPN signifies *to hide* and *to watch*, and צפון TSPUN or SPIN, a *mystery*, an *arcana*, the *north*, a place of darkness. The sphinxes placed at the entrance of the temples guarded the mysteries, by warning those who penetrated into the sanctuaries, that they should conceal a knowledge of them from the profane.

The sphinx, according to Champollion, became successively the particular emblem of each god, and had a special insignia on his forehead (Notice Musée Charles X., p. 114). Did not the priests desire thus to express that all the gods were *hidden* from the people, and that their knowledge, *guarded* in the sanctuaries, was revealed to the initiates only? The name of *Amon*, the great divinity of Egypt, from which all others are but emanations, according to Manetho, signified *hidden*. (*Vide* Champ. Egypt. Panth.)[1]

The sphinx also possessed the signification of *master* or *lord*, principally in the later hieroglyphic texts (Egypt. Gram., p. 27). This signification was given to the sphinx, because in Egypt, as everywhere in the East, the *masters* and *lords* of the people, like the gods, were hidden from their sight.

The Egyptian people venerated the magisterial priests, *because they were permitted to see the king naked.*[2]

Pharaoh delegated his power to Joseph, and named him *interpreter of the sphinx,* צפנת פענח, or *interpreter of hidden things.*[3] The prime minister was the *guardian* and interpreter of the concealed orders of the sovreign, and the secret laws of the empire.

---

[1] The name of Amon, in Hebrew אמן, signifies *faith, truth ;* and אמם or עמם signifies *to hide, to obscure, to veil* (Gesenius) ; thus the name of Amon indicated truth hidden from the people.

[2] See Champollion-Figeac, Ancient Egypt, p. 46.

[3] *Revelator occulti.* See Targ. Syr. Kimchi (Gesenius).

MOLE.

The Egyptians, says Horapollo (II. 63), represented a blind man by a mole, because that animal does not see.

The blind man, spoken of by Horapollo, is the material and worldly man who does not see heavenly things; it is the profane who cannot pierce the veil of the mysteries: such, at least, is the signification given in Hebrew to the mole.

חלד HELD signifies *mole, the world*, and *the duration of life*: מתים מחלד *lovers of worldly things* (Psalm xvii., 14).[1]

When Isaiah says that a man shall cast his idols to the *moles* and to the bats, he employs a symbol to express that man shall renounce his worldly life, and that worship of terrestrial things represented by the *mole* (Isaiah ii., 20).

BULL.

The bull was, according to Horapollo, the sign of the idea *strong, powerful, virile* (Horap. I., 46).

On the Egyptian monuments, in fact, the bull designates *strength* and *power*,[2] and Champollion admits the signification of *husband* (Egypt. Gram., p. 282).

The name of the *ox* or *bull*, אלף or אלוף ALP or ALUP is formed from the root אל AL, signifying *strong, powerful, a hero*. It is on this account that the Hebrew name of the bull אלוף, signifies also a *chief*, a *prince*.[3]

---

[1] There are two homonyms in this phrase, מת signifies *man* and *death*; and חלד *mole* and *world*.

[2] Salvolini, Translation of the Obelisk, p. 8. Leemans on Horapollo, p. 263.

[3] The first letter of the Hebrew alphabet א has the name of the bull; and according to Gesenius, it was at first an image of the head of that animal.

The bull on the obelisk at Paris has the signification given in Hebrew.

This animal was also the symbol of *virility*, of the generative power of nature, and as such represented the Nile, the agent of Egyptian fructification.[1] The bull *Onuphis* was consecrated to Amon, the generator, and the cow *Masre* (generatrix of the sun), to the goddess *Neith*, mother of the god *Phré* (the sun).[2]

In Hebrew the name of the bull פר PR, feminine פרה PRE, is the same word as the verb פרה, *to be fruitful*.

VULTURE.

Horapollo (I. 11) says that the vulture was the symbol of *maternity*,[3] of *heaven*, and *knowledge of the future*, of *mercy*, *Minerva*, and *Juno*.

That author, in commenting on these symbolical attributes, adds that the vulture designated *maternal love*, because it feeds its young with its own blood; he says, a little further on, that the heads of the goddesses and Egyptian queens were ornamented with this bird, which is proved in fact by the monuments (Leemans, Adnot., p. 183).

The vulture represented *heaven*, because, according to Pliny, no one can reach its nest, built on the highest rocks (Nat. Hist., X. 6; Leemans, 172). Which causes Horapollo to say that this bird is begotten by the wind.

It symbolized *knowledge of the future*, because, according to the same author, the ancient kings of Egypt sent augurs on the field of battle, and learned who would

---

[1] Jablonski, Panth. *Apis*.—Rolle, Worship of Bacchus, I., 140–145. Horap. II., 43.

[2] Champollion, Notice du Musée Charles. X., p. 41.

[3] The vulture was specially consecrated to Neith Thermoutis, the mother of the gods and worldly beings (Champ. Notice Musée Charles X., p. 5 and 41).

be the victor and who the vanquished, by watching the side to which the vulture turned : on the monuments the vulture appears on the head of victorious kings (Leemans, 178; Champollion-Figeac, Ancient Egypt, plate xvi.).

Finally, this bird was attributed to *Minerva* and to *Juno*, because, among the Egyptians, Minerva presided in the superior hemisphere and Juno in the inferior hemisphere of the heavens : it would have been absurd, adds Horapollo, to give a masculine representative to the skies which gave birth to the sun, moon, and stars (Horap. I., 11). The Egyptian monuments represent the sky under the figure of a woman bending forward and resting her hands and feet on the earth (Champ. Egypt. Panth.). The monuments also prove that the vulture represented the sky or upper region, the same as upper Egypt (Champ. Egypt. Gram., p. 355 ; Rosetta Inscription, line 10).

The Hebrew confirms the various significations given to the vulture.

The word רחם RHEM, the *vulture*, is thus called says Gesenius, on account of its kindness to its young;[1] in fact, the same word רחם RHEM, is the verb *to love*, having relation particularly to the love of parents for their offspring ; this name also designates maternity and the feminine gender, it signifies the *uterus, woman*, and *young girl.* Would it not appear that the Egyptian was commenting on the Hebrew when he says that the vulture symbolized *maternity?* He adds that this bird represented *mercy* and *heaven ;* and all the nobler passions of the soul are represented by the word רחם RHEM, in the plural רחמים RHEMIM ; it signifies the viscera of the heart and breast, and at the same time *love, piety, mercy,* because it is, in fact, on the viscera of the breast that love and piety act (See Gesenius). The heart and breast, seats of the divine affections, are the two celestial hemispheres over which the *vulture* reigns.

---

[1] Consult Bochart, Hieroz. lib. II., Cap. xxv. and xxvi.; and Didymi Taurinensis, Litteraturæ copticæ rudimentum, p. 9–10.

CHAPTER III.

In the primitive languages, the names of material objects were used to designate abstract ideas corresponding to them; at a later period, a reaction in languages took place, the names of abstract ideas were given to material objects, symbolizing them.

This action and reaction, manifest among those people who have preserved a knowledge of symbols, was one of the causes of the remarkable fact, examples of which are furnished by the Hebrew, that synonyms produce the same homonymies, that is to say, that the different denominations of the same physical object possess the same moral signification; at one time, the abstract idea arising from the symbol, and at another, the name of the symbol being derived from one or more abstract expressions.

It is evident that this fact removes all idea of chance in the formation of symbolic significations and all idea of arbitrary interpretation.

The law which imposed on the synonyms of a language the same homonymies, reproduced the same phenomena in languages foreign to each other, and having nothing

common between them but their symbolic origin. It is
not surprising that we find an explanation of Egyptian
symbols in Hebrew, since I have already shown, in the
history of symbolic colors, that the name of the color
white had the same signification in languages completely
foreign to each other. Thus, the Greek word LEUKOS
signifies *white, happy, agreeable, gay;* in Latin, CANDIDUS,
white, candid, happy; in the German language we find
the words WEISS, *white,* and WISSEN, *to know,* ICH WEISS,
I know; in English WHITE, and WIT, WITTY, WIS-
DOM.

The languages of Greece and Rome, and those of
modern people, altered by numerous admixtures and
long usage, lost the symbolic character, which we find
again in the Hebrew; the application of this last tongue
to Egyptian symbols is a proof of it, confirmed by the
names of the colors.

After the special work published on that subject, it
would appear sufficient to establish that the names of
the colors reproduce in Hebrew the significations assigned to them in our former researches; but it has
appeared to us that it might be useful to make a special
application of this new means of verification to Egyptian
paintings.

WHITE.

The significations given in Hebrew to the color white
designate *purity, candor, nobility.*

חור HEUR, *to be white;* חורים HEURIM, *the noble, the pure,
the white.*

לבן LBN, *to be white; to purge one's self of sin.*

In Egypt the spirits of the dead were clothed in
white like the priests; Phtha, the creator and regenerator, is enclosed in a straight white vestment, symbol of
the egg from which he was born.[2] The egg called to
mind the birth of the world and the new birth, or regeneration of the *pure* or the *white*

---

[1] Symbolic Colors of Antiquity, the Middle Ages, and Modern
Times, pp. 50 and 51.
[2] See Paintings of the Funereal Ritual; and Emeric-David, *Vul-
ain.*

RED.

The names of this color are formed from those of fire, and, in their turn, they form those of love. Thus, ארגון ARGUN, *purple*, is formed by ארה ARE, *to burn*.

ארגמן ARGMN, another name of purple, is also formed of ארה ARE, *to burn*, and of רגם RGM, which signifies to *color*, to *paint*, to *conjoin*, and a *friend*.

Red, the most glaring of all colors, was used to designate the verbs *to color* and *paint*, and, as the image of fire, it designated love, the *universal tie of beings*.

The names of man and woman were borrowed from fire and the color red, because the physical, the moral, and religious life of humanity spring from love: איש AISCH, *man*, from the root אש ASCH, *fire*, אשה ASCHE, *woman* and *fire*.

אדם ADM, *man* and *the color red*.

On Egyptian monuments all the men have the flesh painted red, and women yellow; in like manner the gods have the flesh red and goddesses yellow; at least, when these divinities have not a color specially attributed to them. We see, in this fact, a confirmation of the Hebrew signification of man, whose name signifies *red*; we shall presently show why the feminine gender is designated by *yellow*.

YELLOW.

Among the Egyptians, as among the Hebrews, fire was the symbol of divine life, of human life, and of the life that animates all created beings.

The inward essence of divinity was considered by the Egyptians as male and female.[1] The *heat of the fire* represented the universal male principle. The *light of the fire* was the female principle.

Le Pimandre, who, according to Champollion, has preserved to us, at least in part, the doctrines of Egypt,[2] reveals this mystery to us.

[1] Symbolic Colors, p. 105. Consult Champ. Egypt. Panth., *Amon*, and *female Amon*.

[2] "The hermetic books, says Champollion, notwithstanding the opinions hazarded by certain modern critics, contain a mass of purely Egyptian traditions always found to agree with the monuments."—Egyptian Pantheon, Art. *Thoth trismégiste*.

Thought, says Hermes, is God, male and female ; for it is *light and life* (Pimandre, cap. I., sec. 9). It is evident that life, in opposition to light, designates the ardor of the fire and the male principle, as light symbolizes the female principle.

I have elsewhere shown that red was the symbol of the *heat of the fire*, and yellow, that of *light*. In like manner, in the Hebrew language, the name of the color red is formed of that of fire, and the name of yellow, or gold color, צהב TSEB, designates an emanation or radiation of light, as its proper signification indicates to *shine*, to be *resplendent*.

The necessary consequence of the preceding is, that the male principle, symbolized by ardent fire, must have been represented by red, and the female principle, being identified with the idea of light, must have been painted yellow. Pimandre also explains the singular fact that, on the Egyptian monuments, men have their flesh painted red, and women yellow.

Champollion-Figeac thinks that difference comes from the women having been of a lighter complexion than the men (Ancient Egypt, p. 29). Under this hypothesis, we should conceive various shades of complexion ; but it would be impossible to explain why the men are painted *cherry-red*, and the women *lemon-yellow*, as represented by Champollion the younger, in his Egyptian Grammar, p. 8, and in his Egyptian Pantheon, and as the monuments lead us to believe.

The vignette at the head of this chapter represents Athor, the Egyptian Venus, in the solar disc.[1] Athor, wife of Phtha, or of *fire*, is the divinity of *beauty* and *light;* her name signifies *dwelling of Horus* (Plut. De Iside) ; her color is *yellow.*

On the Anaglyphs, the solar disc is painted red or yellow, and sometimes red, surrounded by a yellow stripe. On a monument published by Champollion, the rising sun is represented by a yellow disc, and the setting sun by a red one, bordered with yellow (Egyptian Pantheon, *Ré*).

---

[1] Description of Ancient Egypt, vol. IV., plate xxiii., cornice of the great Temple of Denderah.

BLUE.

The name of this color does not appear to exist in Hebrew, at least, not that I know of;[1] but its signification is preserved to us in that of sapphire.

The name of sapphire, the same in Hebrew as in French, ספיר SPIR or SPHIR is formed by the root ספר SPR or SPHR, signifying *to write, to speak, celebrate, praise,* a *scribe, writing,* the *book.*

These various significations indicate the *Divine voice,* the written or spoken word, the wisdom of God, contained in the *sepher* of the Hebrews, or the Bible.

Sapphire is the color of the Egyptian god, *Amon,* whose name, preserved in the Bible exactly as in the hieroglyphic legends, אמון AMUN, or אמן AMN, signifies, in Hebrew, *truth, wisdom,* as his color, sapphire, ספיר, indicates the Divine word, spoken or written.

The chief of the Egyptian Hierogrammats wore on his breast a sapphire, on which was engraved a representation of the goddess of *truth* and *justice,* Thme, whose name תם THM, or תמה THME, signifies, in Hebrew, *justice* and *truth* (See Art. *Ostrich Feather*).

The High Priest of the Hebrews wore on his breast a stone, having the same name; *truth* and *justice,* תמים THMIM.

HYACINTH.

The Hebrew name of this color is תכלת THKLTH,[2] formed of the root תכלה THKLE, signifying *absolution, perfection, hope* and *constancy,* absolutio, perfectio, spes, fiducia (Gesenius); תכלית THKLITH, *perfection, consummation.*

In the work on symbolic colors, it will be found that the hyacinth was the symbol of *perfection, hope* and con*stancy* in spiritual combats.

This color does not appear to have been employed on the Egyptian monuments.

[1] שחר signifies black, and, probably, a dark blue. The word תכלת designates hyacinth, or bluish purple.

[2] תכלת *hyacinthus* (Robertson, Thesaurus), purpura cerulea, sericum flavum (Gesenius).

GREEN.

The Hebrew name of *green* is ירק IRQ, *viridis*, which also signifies *verdure, green grass*.

This word comes from the roots ירה IRE, *to found, to regulate ;* and of רק RQ, *space ;* רקח RQE, *time, expansion of space ;* רקיע the *firmament*.

Thus, the name of green designates the beginning of time, the creation of the world, the birth of everything that exists. This is the meaning given to *green* in the work on ,symbolic colors, and which is also constantly given to it on the Egyptian monuments.

The god Phtha, founder of the world, the creator and upholder, has always green flesh.

PHTHA, says Champollion, *is the active creating spirit, the divine intelligence, who undertook, in the beginning, the accomplishment of the universe, in all truth, and with supreme art.* (Egypt. Panth., see Jamblich. De Mysteriis, sec. viii., cap. viii.) His flesh, adds the learned Frenchman, is always painted green.

This divinity holds in his hand a sceptre, surmounted by four cornices, which, in hieroglyphic writing, is the symbol of *coördination* (Champ. Egypt. Panth.) ; and the root ירה signifies to *institute*, instituere, conformare (Gesenius). This sceptre is painted of the four colors attributed to the four elements—the red, denoting fire ; blue, air ; green, water ; and the brown-yellow, or russet, sand or earth. (See Emeric-David, *Vulcain*, p. 65.)

Green was attributed to water, because, in Egyptian cosmogony, water was the primitive agent of creation (Champ. Panth., *Cnouphis-Nilus*). The word ירה IRE, root of the name of green, signifies, *to place the foundation*, and *to sprinkle*.

Phtha is not only the creator of the world, but the regenerator or spiritual creator of man ; under the form of Phtha-Socari, he rules the destinies of souls that abandon earthly bodies, to be distributed in the thirty-two superior regions. His flesh is also green (Champ. Panth., plate xi.).

The signification of green, arising from its name, and its attribution to the god-creator of the world, it is easy to make its applications to other divinities.

The god *Tore*, or *Thra*, the *world personified*, is represented sitting in an ark floating on the *green* waters of cosmogony (Champ. Egypt. Panth.).

The god *Lunus* (the moon), whose flesh is green, is also represented sitting in a bark, or *bari*, floating in green waters. The god Lunus was, doubtless, a cosmographic divinity, since he appears with the emblems of Phtha, the sceptre of coördination in his hand. The Hebrew name of the moon, ירה IRHE, is formed of one of the roots of green, ירה IRE, which signifies to *found*, to *regulate*, instituere, conformare (Gesenius).

The same root, ירה IRE, signifies, also, to *instruct*, and to *sprinkle*. We have seen, in the article *Dew*, that this symbol designated the sacred doctrine. Thoth, the god-creator of men, founder of the social state, the god of science, of the sacred doctrine, and the *hierogrammats*, has his flesh painted green on two monuments copied in Champollion's Egyptian Pantheon. Thoth pours over the head of the neophyte the waters of purification, symbol of celestial dew. (See the representation of Egyptian baptism, at the commencement of this work.)

Netphe, mother of the gods, lady of heaven, as she is called in the legend of that divinity, is often represented in the midst of the tree Persea, pouring the divine beverage over souls; her *flesh is green*.

Finally, Neith with the lion's head, called Pascht, represents the regenerating principle, under the emblem of vigilance and moral power, the *lion;* she grasps, with both hands, the great serpent Apop, enemy of the gods, and symbol of the wicked and impious. The inscription accompanying this image of the divinity is: *Powerful Pascht, eye of the sun, sovereign of power, directress of all the gods, chastising the unclean.*

The three different forms under which she is represented in Champollion's Pantheon, all show her with *green flesh.*

Pascht, protectress of warriors, represented, according to the French philologist, the wisdom that gives the *victory* (Pantheon).

Green was the symbol of victory (Symbolic Colors, p. 215). In the Funereal Ritual, the serpent pierced by the swords of the gods appears in a *green* enclosure.

Neith is again manifested under the form of the god

dess *Seben*, the Egyptian Lucina, who presided at childbirth ; she is represented, in Champollion's Pantheon,
under three different forms, and always with *green flesh*.

Green symbolized material birth and being spiritually
born again. According to a long preserved symbolic
tradition, *the emerald hastened childbirth* (Symbolic Colors,
p. 214), and the Egyptian Lucina is of emerald color.

The symbology of green, of which we have here
given but a slight sketch, predominates in the religious
monuments of Egypt ; the reason is, that it taught the
very foundation of the mysteries of initiation ; that is, the
birth of the world, and the moral creation of neophytes.

BROWN-RED, or RUSSET.

The name of the color russet, הֵמוּץ HEMUTS, signifies
the *oppressor*, the *violent*, ruber, oppressor, violentus
(Rosenmüller, Vocab.). We have seen that the word
was formed from חֵם HEM, *devouring heat ;* חוּם HEUM, *black*
(see Article *Crocodile*). Thus this word perfectly corre-
sponds to the color red-black, attributed, according to
Plutarch and Diodorus, to the spirit of *oppression* and *violence*, to Seth or Typhon (Symbolic Colors, p. 257). The
concubine of Typhon, Thoueri, is represented in a painting in Champollion's Egyptian Pantheon with her flesh
russet-color.

קדר QDR, *brown*, *russet*, pullus subniger, signifies, in
addition, *filthy, to be in affliction*, and *Ishmaelites* (Gesenius).

BLACK.

There are two shades of black existing in symbology,
one the opposite of red, the other of white (Symbolic
Colors, p. 167).

The first designates ignorance arising from evil and
all selfish or hateful passions. The second indicates
ignorance of mind, not confirmed by wickedness of heart,
and seeking to leave that state of intellectual death.

Black from red (red-black) is called in Hebrew חוּם
HEUM, as shown in the Article on *Russet*. This name
forms the word חוּמָה HEUME, *an enclosing wall*, because

evil and falsity bind man as in a strait place (consult Art. *Ass*).

Black from white, in Hebrew שחר SCHHER. *black*, signifies, in addition, *the dawn* and *to seek*. This word, the connection of which with the name of white, צחר TSHER, appears evident, designates the expectation of the profane, who seeks and sees shine the first light of dawn. The black Osiris, who appears at the commencement of the Funereal Ritual, represents that state of the soul which, from the midst of darkness surrounding the earth, passes into the world of light.

The same indication belongs, in the judgment of the soul, to the two children of Osiris, Anubis and Horus, who weigh the soul in the scales of Amenti.   Anubis, the god of the dead and of embalming, is black, and Horus red and yellow (Description of Egypt).

Thoth Psychopompe, conductor of souls to the presence of Osiris, has the head of the black Ibis.

CHAPTER IV.

THE principle of Bible symbols is taught by the words of our Lord to the apostle Simon, who had just acknowledged him as the Christ, the Son of the living God :

Thou art Peter, and on this rock will I build my church (Matthew xvi. 18).[1]

Stone is the symbol of faith ; the foundation of the Christian faith is the recognition of Jesus as the Christ, the Son of the living God.

Jesus gave to Simon the surname of *Peter* (stone)— (Mark iii. 16)—because the divine mission that apostle had to perform represented, spiritually, what is materially represented by the corner-stone of an edifice.

It cannot be necessary to say to Christians that the Messiah did not play on the word, but expressed, by a symbol, the functions that Peter would have to represent

---

[1] The word *pierre*, in French, signifies both *Peter* (a proper name) and *stone*. This latter signification is the one intended to be given by Portal, as will be seen by the context.— *Translator.*

and accomplish. We must choose between the two interpretations—one trivial and the other sublime ; the first presenting a pun, to speak plainly, the second affording a key to Bible symbols (see the word *Stone* hereafter).

The system of homonyms applied to the interpretation of the Bible is not new, though no scholar has made it the object of special study ; this principle is so evidently employed by the inspired writers, that Hebraists cannot fail to recognize it in some passages.

It is more than two hundred years since the celebrated Heinsius, in the extended preface to his *Aristarchus sacer*, proved that the Gospel of St. John, written in Greek, had been conceived in Syriac, because, in that Gospel, the inspired writer alludes to the double meanings of words—double meanings that exist only in Syriac and not in Greek.[1] The learned commentator makes the same observation, after an examination of the word ἀρετή, used by St. Peter in his Second Epistle, chap. i., v. 5.[2]

I take these two citations of Heinsius from Goulianof's work on Egyptian Archæology (III., 560). The Russian academician follows them with these reflections : " It was, then, by the discovery of homonymies in the obscure and difficult passages that the celebrated critic became convinced of this important condition of the exegesis, to

[1] Si quis ex me quærat, quanam lingua scripserit evangelista noster ; hellenistica scripsisse dicam. Si quis, qua conceperit qui scripsit ; syriacam fuisse dicam. Ad eam autem quod est hellenistis proprium, et voces et sermonem deflexisse græcum : quare ad allusiones, non quæ extant, sed quas animo conceperat, eundem esse ; nihil enim æque atque has amat Oriens : Statim initio, καὶ τὸ φῶς ἐν τῇ σκοτίᾳ φαίνει, καὶ ἡ σκοτία αὐτὸ οὐ κατέλαβεν, dicitur. Quod si chaldaice aut syriace efferas, suavissimam allusionem, quam hec græca, nec hellenistica admittit lingua, protinus agnosces. Nam τὸ קבל *cabbel* est καταλαμβάνειν, קבל *cebal* antem ἡ σκοτία, קבל enim Thargumistis *obscurari*. Quantopere autem hos amaverit evangelista, passim jam ostendimus.

(Consult Goulianof, Archéologie égyptienne, III., p. 560.)

[2] Igitur, ut jam dicebam, alia lingua primo concipit quæ scribit, alia, quæ jam concepit, hellenista exprimit. Primo enim ad originem ipsius linguæ respicit, qua sua exprimit, aut ejus sequitur interpretes. Et quia quæ diversis concipi ac scribi solent, non conveniunt ubique (nam ut litteræ ac syllabæ, sic et allusiones ac paronomasiæ, quæ singulis sunt propriæ, transfundi commode vix possunt), de his ipsis ex interprete earum lingua ferri sententia ac judicari potest. Utrum, nempe, hebræa aliquid conceptum fuerit an syra ; nam in eo quod eadem scriptum ac conceptum, nulla difficultas. (Ibid. *just before*.)

4

wit: that the authors of the New Testament often employed, not the proper word expressing their idea, *but
the equivalent of the Shemitic word*, of which the *honomym*
contained that idea, either in Syriac, Chaldaic, or Hebrew.
Solomon Glassius, in his *Philologia Sacra*, in the chapter
on PARONOMASES, cites many examples of homonyms in
support of the distinguished commentator's discovery,
and says: *Quandoque vocum παρήχησις et allusio in alia
lingua quam ea, qua scripsit auctor sanctus quærenda est.*"
(Philologia Sacra.   Lipsiæ, 1713, p. 1996.)

"And finally," says Goulianof, " we will cite the interesting prefatory dissertation of the learned commentator, Michaëlis, devoted exclusively to the examination
of *sacred paronomases*, in the Old as well as in the New
Testament.   After having indicated the expressions
brought together, or employed in the same phrase on
account of their *consonance*, the author takes up the fact
of *tacit homonyms*, to the examination of which he devotes
several paragraphs ; and the reflections with which he
accompanies each article, either of these last, or *explicit
paronomases*, sufficiently prove that the learned author,
far from seeing a play on words in them, on the contrary, considered them as a class of expressions intimately connected with the usages of sacred writing.
Such is also the opinion of the celebrated Glassius,
whom we have just cited; an opinion in which the
commentators will, doubtless, concur, when they become
certain that silent homonyms furnish a key to the
enigma, and act as SPIRITUAL LEGENDS *to all allegories, all
parables, and all symbolic language;* that in the homonyms
alone is to be sought an explanation of the mysteries
of the Scriptures, whenever the letter presents a difficulty in the exegesis ; that, in a word, the TACIT HOMO
NYMS constitute the *spirit of the Scriptures*, and serve as
TYPES to the mystic language of the *letter*, the conditional value of which disappears in proportion as their
corresponding terms are appreciated." (Goulianof, Archéologie égyptienne, tom. III., p. 563.)

I adopt the principle of the learned Academician of
Petersburgh, but am astonished at the deduction he
draws, when he says that we should look in vain for
these homonyms in the Shemitic dialects (III., p. 569),
and pretends to explain the figures of the Bible by the

Coptic language, which he confounds with the sacred language of Egypt. "It remains for us," says he, "to notice a superficial objection, which would, however, be favorable to the present question. Among the hagiographs of the Old Testament, nearly all the prophets had never been in Egypt, and could not have been acquainted with the sacred language of that country; this objection becomes still more positive with regard to the evangelists and apostles. How, then, it will be said, should we conceive the possibility of explaining, by means of the *sacred language* of Egypt, the words of the prophets, and those of the evangelists and apostles, who had no knowledge of that language? Now, if the use of that language will lead us to an understanding of the *spiritual meaning of the Scriptures*, this fact will become a demonstration in a measure material to the revelation of the mysteries of the new covenant, and of the inspiration of the hagiographs." (Ibid., p. 557.)

In order to consider the Coptic as containing the spiritual meaning of the Bible, it would, in the first place, be necessary that that language should explain the symbols of Egypt, which we deny in presence of the facts known to science; it would further be necessary, by a comparison of all the passages in the Bible, containing the same word, to show that this word has, in reality, the double meaning assigned to it; now, with Mr. Goulianof's method, this appears impossible to us.

It is evident to us that, if the prophets concealed their mysteries in the double meaning of words, those words were taken from the language understood by them. It is also clear, that if, without the knowledge even of the prophets themselves, Divine inspiration concealed the spiritual meaning under the double meaning of a letter, then, in the Hebrew letter must we find the secret thought of Biblical figures, and not in the Coptic, or vulgar Egyptian, scarcely capable of explaining the symbols of its own country.

Besides, the passage from Clemens Alexandrinus fully proves that the symbols of the Egyptians were like those of the Hebrews. Mr. Goulianof pretends, on the contrary, that the Hebrew symbols were similar to those of the Egyptians; he consequently finds himself in opposition to modern science, and the only passage from an ancient author competent to explain the question.

We in nowise pretend that all the exegetical difficulties of the Bible may be removed by the means we offer; we are not, above all, foolish enough to think that, by this means, we may open the book of life, and break its seals; but we simply think that healthy criticism, before depriving itself of this method of investigation, should conscientiously study it, and only admit or reject it after submitting it to the proofs of which it is susceptible.

I will not seek to explain, in this place, how the spiritual meaning may be hidden under the double meaning of a letter; I study and only desire to establish the fact itself.

The symbolic meaning is not always clearly manifested in the sacred text. Wherefore, to arrive at the signification of a symbol, it is not sufficient to interpret it as we meet it in a passage from the Bible, but we must reconstruct its signification by considering all its names. The proof of the truth of this rule appears from the fact that the New Testament is partly written in a symbolic manner, as proved by Revelations, the twenty-fourth chapter of Matthew, etc., etc.; and that the Greek is not a symbolic language; the symbols of the Bible must, then, allude to all the Hebrew synonyms answering to the Greek word to be interpreted; since the Greek is to be translated into Hebrew, there is no greater reason for choosing an expression than its synonym.

The inspired writer in the Old Testament seems, designedly, to veil his thoughts under words that evidently have not the double meaning he attributes to them. If the Psalmist says that *the righteous man shall flourish like the palm-tree*, צדיק כתמר יפרח, he does not employ the expression תם THM, *the just man*, to compare him to the palm-tree, תמר THMR, but he expresses this idea by a synonym that does not produce the same homonymy, צדיק TSDIQ, *the just man*.

It will be understood that, if, in the Bible, a symbol had always been placed in relation with its homonym, the mystery surrounding the sacred text would have been divulged. Like Fabre d'Olivet, we need not, therefore, endeavor to explain a Bible phrase by itself.

by scrutinizing the moral sense of each word or its roots, for, by this method, we should arrive at no useful or scientific result.

The method I recommend for interpreting the Bible, is that I have just applied to Egyptian symbols; to reconstruct, in the first place, the meaning of each symbol by the moral significations of its different names, and, by its application to various passages of the Bible, ascertain that the symbol really possesses such signification. This method, adopted for interpreting the monuments of Egypt, ought to produce the same results in the exegesis of the sacred book.

A few words may here be addressed to those Christians who might be fearful lest our faith should be injured by companionship with Egypt. Science can never injure the Christian religion, they both descend from the source of all truth; if the system now presented is true, it will furnish new proof of the divine inspiration of the Bible, if false, religion has nothing to fear from it.

Already, among Protestants, the Rev. Mr. Coquerel ad shown the importance Egyptian studies might have on the exegesis of the Bible : " Of all people," said he, " the Egyptians had the most intercourse with the Hebrews, from the journey of Abraham (Gen., xii, 10) to the carrying away of Jeremiah, (Jer., xliii. 6.) that is, from the first Patriarch to the fall of Jerusalem. The name of Egypt is the foreign one most frequently met with in the Scriptures; the distinctive sign of the elect was, perhaps, worn by the Egyptian priesthood ;[1] Moses was learned in all their wisdom (Acts, vii. 22) ; Solomon married a daughter of their kings (I. Kings, iii. 1) ; and what adds to the interest of this question is, that Israel was forbidden to hold communication with the neighboring nations ; one people only being excepted from this interdiction, and that people was the Egyptians (Deut., xxiii. 7). All this leads us to presume that the best commentary on Jewish Antiquities was sculptured on the Pharaonic temples, palaces and obelisks ; but those terrible hieroglyphics seemed forever to separate the Jordan and the Nile."[2]

[1] *Vide* Art. *Ant*, p. 35, circumcision of the Egyptian priests.
[2] Letter on Champollion's hieroglyphic system, considered in its rela-

The labor of the Protestant minister was not lost to science. The Abbé Greppo, Vicar-General of Belley, understood its applications, and, seeing the truth, without fear openly published it. Collecting the numerous Bible phrases that seemed to have been copied from the monuments of Egypt, he says : " The great number of dates which have been read up to this time in the hieroglyphic, hieratic or demotic inscriptions of the papyrus, etc., are always written after the same formula, and in nowise differ from the style in which they are usually expressed in the sacred books : *In the fifth year, the fifth day of the month* . . . ., *by command of the king of the obedient people* (the titles, given and surnames of the Prince). Is not this similarity of expression striking?

" There exist, perhaps, more prominent ones in the titles of honor given to the princes and gods, and collected by Champollion in his *Tableau général.* Several of these formulas of public acts detail religious ideas which we should in vain seek for on the monuments of antiquity, whether Greek or Roman, but which predominate in the simple and noble style of the Scriptures Such are those of *cherished*[1] *of Ammon* (Jupiter), entirely similar to *dilectus a Domino suo Samuel* (Eccle., xlvi. 13), *approved of Phtah* (Vulcan), *tried of Re* (the sun), analogous expressions to *acceptus Deo, probatus Deo,* often met with in the Scriptures. The lords gods, identical, with the exception of being in the plural, with *Dominus Deo* in the Bible ; *great and grand,* quality ascribed to *Thoth,* the Egyptian Mercury, and which reminds us of the *sanctus, sanctus, sanctus,* which, in our sublime prophets, the heavenly choirs are ever singing at the foot of the throne of the Eternal."[2]

I shall not follow Mr. Greppo in other similar resemblances, these will suffice to show that the Bible and

tions to the Holy Scriptures, by Coquerel ; Amsterdam, 1825, p. 6-7.

[1] It has often been remarked that the pagan antiquities seldom speak of the love due to the Deity. Among the Egyptians, the expressions *cherished of the gods, loving the gods,* are frequently repeated, and seem to indicate more correct ideas of Divinity and the duties imposed by it on man (Note of the Abbé Greppo).

[2] Essay on the hieroglyphic system of Champollion the younger, and its advantages to Scripture criticism, by Greppo Paris, Dondey-Dupré, 1829.

the Egyptian monuments mutually aid in their interpretation, and that the enlightened critic of our day cannot put aside the advantages arising from an attentive examination and comparison of the hieroglyphic monuments, and the book and language of the Hebrew prophet, of *Moses, learned in the wisdom of the Egyptians* (Acts, vii. 22).

I shall not here depend on the resemblance existing between the Hebrew and the Coptic, as shown by Dr. Lowe,[1] nor on the more decisive relations which unite the sacred language of the Jews with the sacred language of the Egyptians; I will content myself with presenting some examples of the application of our theory to the symbols of the Bible; the greater part of those of the Egyptians, examined in Chapter II., have manifested their application to the Bible, and I only purpose in this place to furnish a new aid to the exegesis and not a treatise on the subject.

STONE.

Stone and rock, on account of their hardness and use, became the symbol of a firm and stable foundation.

In Hebrew the generic name of stones and rocks is אבן ABN, a word which, according to Gesenius, signifies also, *to construct, to build,* and which he also identifies with the root אמן AMN, an *architect, truth,* and *faith;* thence, אמנה AMNE, a *column,* and *truth.*

Fortified by the interpretation of one of the most celebrated Hebraists of Germany, we may consider the *stone* as the symbol of *faith* and *truth.*

Christ said to Simon, who had just acknowledged him as the Son of the living God: Thou art Peter, and on this rock will I build my church[2] (Matthew, xvi. 18).

Christ teaches the very principle of symbology when naming *Peter* he who represented *faith,* or the foundation of the Church.

---

[1] The origin of the Egyptian language proved by the analysis of that and the Hebrew, by Dr. Lowe; London, 1837. Consult Didymi Taurinensis, Litteraturæ copticæ rudimentum; Parmæ, 1783.

[2] כף *rock,* כיפא Chald., whence the Greek name of Peter, *Κηφᾶς,* Cephas; the word כף rock, also signifies *the sole of the feet,* basis of man.

In the Bible, precious stones have particularly the signification of *truth;* the Revelations of St. John furnish numerous examples.

On Egyptian monuments, precious stones are called *hard stones of truth* (Champ. Egypt. Gram., p. 100).

In opposition to this signification of truth and faith, there is given to stone, in the Bible and in Egypt, the signification of *error* and *impiety,* and among these two peoples it was attributed to the infernal genius, the foundation of all falsity.[1]

The name of Seth or Typhon, the principle of evil and error in Egyptian Theogony, is always accompanied by a symbolic sign; this sign, according to Champollion's Grammar (p. 100), is the *stone.* *Seth* (Champ. Gram., p. 114).

The name of the Egyptian divinity is also set down in the Bible, since the hieroglyphic group gives in Hebrew characters the word שׁט scht, *sin,* which forms the name of Satan, שׂטן schtn. This name *Satan* signifies in Hebrew the *adversary,* the *enemy;* now, one of the Hebrew names of *stone* has the additional signification of the *adversary,* the *enemy,* צר tsr, *lapis, adversarius, hostis* (Gesenius).

The stone specially consecrated to Seth or Typhon was the *hewn stone,* and it had, in the language of the monuments, the name of *Seth,* to the exclusion of all others which are called anr (Champ. Gram., p. 100). Truth was symbolized by the hard stone, and error by the soft one, that may be hewn.

The particular determinative of the stone *Seth* was the

knife placed above the sign representing the stone.[2]

The Hebrew again explains this group, inexplicable by the Coptic; the word צר tsr, signifies a *stone,* an *enemy,*

---

[1] For rule of oppositions, see work on Symbolic Colors, p. 32.

[2] Champollion translates this group by *calcareous stone;* the word *Seth* is not in the Coptic; we must depend on the group itself, which signifies *cut, hewn stone,* the knife being in the Egyptian grammar the determinative of the ideas of *division* and *separation* (Champ. Egypt. Gram., p. 384).

and a *knife*, and forms the word צור TSUR, *to cut, to hew*, and *a stone*.

Jehovah says in Exodus: *If thou wilt make me an altar, thou shalt not build it of hewn stone; if thou lift the knife* (or chisel) *upon it, thou hast polluted it* (Exod. xx. v. 22 in the Hebrew, 25 in the translations).

Joshua built an altar of stones, which the chisel had not touched (Joshua, viii. 30, 31).

The Temple of Jerusalem was built of whole stones, and the sound of axe, hammer, nor any tool of iron was not heard during the building (1 Kings, vi. 7, which is the III. of the Vulgate).

POTTER.

Isaiah says: *O, Lord, thou art our Father; we are the clay, and thou our potter; and we all are the work of thy hand* (Is. lxiv. 8).

There being no difficulty in understanding this passage, it will be easy to see in it the application of the principle we have established.

The word employed by Isaiah is יצר ITSR, which signifies a *potter*, and the *creator of the world*.

Job (xvii. 7) calls the *members of the human body* יצרי, properly *potter's mouldings*.

And the name of man אדם ADM, Adam, is formed of that of clay or red earth אדמה ADME.

Thus, the Hebrew language gives, in a positive manner, the signification of a symbol or image, about which there can be no misapprehension.

Egypt here confirms our system: *On the bas-reliefs at Philæ*, says Salvolini, *we see the god Chnouphis, the former, making human limbs in a potter's mill, charged with clay* (Analysis of Egyptian texts, p. 24, No. 76).

Champollion gives in his Grammar the image of *Kneph Potter* (p. 283 and 348). We reproduce one of the variants of that symbol.

4*

PALM-TREE.

The palm-tree was the symbol of *truth, justice*, and *integrity*, since its name תמר THMR, the *palm-tree*, the *palm*, is formed of that of תם THM, *integrity, justice*, and *truth*, ἀλήθεια.

The Psalmist says : *The righteous shall flourish like the palm-tree.* (Ps. xcii. 12, trans. from the Vulgate xci. 13).

In the Apocalypse, the righteous carry palms in their hands (vii. 9).

When Jesus came to Jerusalem to attend the feast, the Jews took palm-branches and went before him, crying : Blessed be he who comes in the Name of the Lord (John xii. 13).

HORSE.

The horse is the symbol of intelligence ; man should govern his mind as the rider guides his horse.

This results from the Hebrew, since the name of the saddle-horse, פרש PRSCH, further signifies *to explain, to define, to give intelligence* (Gesenius, Rosenmüller).

The same result is obtained from the Bible, which translates *rider* by wisdom and *horse* by understanding, in a passage where, speaking of the Ostrich, it says : *God hath deprived her of wisdom, neither hath he imparted to her understanding ; what time she lifteth up herself on high, she scorneth the* HORSE *and his* RIDER (Job xxxix. 17, 18).

Ye shall be filled at my table with horses and chariots, says Ezekiel (xxxix. 20).

Come and gather yourselves together unto the supper of the great God, that ye may eat the flesh of horses and them that sit on them, says the Apocalypse (xix. 17, 18).

Who does not see here that there can be no question of eating horses, chariots, and riders, but to become filled with a knowledge of divine truth ? the rider represents wisdom which guides the understanding, the chariot indicates religious doctrine.

The understanding of man, not kept within bounds by wisdom, is designated in the following passages :

The Lord delighteth not in the strength of the horse (Ps cxlvii. 10).

An horse is a vain thing for safety (Ps. xxxiii. 17).

The Lord will make Judah as his goodly horse in the attle; and the riders on horses shall be confounded (Zach. x. 3 to 5.)

Thus the horse represents the understanding of man which is elevated toward God, or is abased in descending toward matter; this state it is which is specially designated in this passage : *Be ye not as the horse or as the mule, which have no understanding* (Ps. xxxii. 9).

The *race-horse*, the *vigorous courser* is called רכש RKSCH, a word which also signifies *to acquire, to appropriate*, because the mind of man, traversing the field of intelligence, *acquires* fresh knowledge.

LAMB.

In the first chapter of the Gospel of St. John we are taught that the Messiah was the *Word*, or the *word of God;* the forerunner seeing Jesus coming towards him, cried out : *Behold the Lamb of God, which taketh away the sins of the world* (John i. 29).

The name of the *lamb* אמר AMR, (Chald.) is in Hebrew that of the *Word* or second person of the Trinity.

The Word was made flesh among us, to take away the sins of the world and to overcome the kingdom of evil, and the word כבש KBSCH, signifies a *lamb, to beget*, and *to put under foot* (Gesenius).

SUN AND MOON.

The sun warming and lighting the body of man was the symbol of Divinity, which inflames the heart and reveals itself to the understanding ; such is the teaching of the Hebrew language, and the Bible uses it in this sense.

The name of the *sun* and of *light* אור AUR, signifies *revelation* and *doctrine* (Gesenius).

The moon, which, according to the Egyptian priests, *is lighted by the sun and receives from it her vital power*,[1] became the symbol of faith which reflects revealed truths;

---

[1] Eusèbe, Præpar. evangel. lib. III. cap. xii. Consult. Champ. Panthéon égyptien, Art. *Pooh.*

it was on this account that the name of the moon ירה IRHE, formed the verb ירה IRE, *to learn, to teach.*

In Egypt, teaching the truths of the faith, was represented by the *dew* or *rain* (Horap. I. 37); and the same word ירה IRE signifies to *sprinkle, to throw drops of water.* In the representations of Egyptian baptism, the two personages who pour the waters of divine life and purity on the head of the neophyte, symbolize the *sun* and *moon*, or Horus with the hawk's head, and Thoth-Lunus with the head of an Ibis.[1]

And finally, as faith is the foundation of the church, the same verb ירה signifies *to found, to lay the angular corner-stone* (Gesenius).

We deduce from these observations that the sun is the revelation of the wisdom and love of God, and that the moon is the symbol of faith. Let us apply these significations to a few obscure passages in the Bible.

At the command of Joshua, the sun stands still on Gibeon, and the moon in the valley of Ajalon (Joshua, x. 12). I am not about to discuss the question of the miracle, I seek only the hidden meaning of this passage: the sun stopping signifies the presence of divine love, which inflames the hearts of men; the moon stopping designates the presence of faith, that enlightens and fortifies the mind. Is not this exclamation, taken by Joshua from the book of Jaschar (Jos. x. 13), an invocation to the Divine love to animate the hearts of the combatants, and to faith to give strength to his arms?

A passage from Isaiah proves the truth of this interpretation:

Thy sun shall no more go down, says the prophet, *neither shall thy moon withdraw itself; for the Lord shall be thine everlasting light, and the days of thy mourning shall be ended.* (Isaiah, lx. 20).

The sun stopping manifests the presence of God; in opposition, the sun going down designates the absence of the Deity, as shown by the following passages: *And it shall come to pass in that day, saith the Lord God, that I will cause the sun to go down at noon* (Amos, viii. 9).

Jeremiah says: *She that hath borne seven children, shall give up the ghost, her sun shall go down while it is yet day* (Jer. xv. 9).

[1] See Art. *Dew.*

In the Bible, the sun has sometimes a signification of evil omen, of *devouring heat*, *fury*, *selfishness*, which is explained by the word חמה HEME, *the sun*, *heat of the sun*, *anger* (Gesenius); a meaning also found in the name of the *crocodile*, formed from the root חם HEM (see Art. *Crocodile*).

Job commends himself for not having worshiped the sun and moon (xxxi. 26), that is, for not having been perverse and selfish, and for not having had faith in his own wisdom; there is no question of Sabianism in this passage, but of the two fundamental principles of man's spiritual life, *love* and *intelligence*.

ABOUT THE AUTHOR

Baron Frederic de Portal (1804-1876) Born into a minor noble family from the Languedoc who could trace their ancestry back to the early medieval period. They were active during the wars of the Albigensian Crusade, although they seem to have opposed the French for local patriotic reasons rather than for their beliefs. But dissent did run in their blood and with the coming of the Reformation they embraced the Protestant faith, although after the collapse of the Huguenot cause some of the family fled to England. Frédéric's branch, however, remained in South-Western France and, as a Jurist, historian and author, he became, perhaps, the most distinguished head of his family. He wrote one other book on symbolism, but it is for Des Couleurs Symboliques (1837) – which was utilised by Eliphas Lévi in his studies of the Kabbalah – that he is deservedly best known.